THE ESSENTIAL ALKALINE DIET RECIPES

2 Books In 1: Explore 50+ Delicious Recipes and a Perfect Meal Plan to Lose Weight, Increase Energy and Heal Your Body with The Essential Alkaline Diet Recipes.

BY

Warwick Doyle

THE ESSENTIAL ALKALINE DIET RECIPES FOR BEGINNERS

THE ESSENTIAL ALKALINE RECIPES FOR BEGINNERS

THE ESSENTIAL ALKALINE DIET RECIPES FOR BEGINNERS

Table of Contents

INTRODUCTION

Alkaline diet can help us in many ways. The accentuation on leafy foods that is at the center of alkaline diets offers the guarantee of solid weight reduction. No uncommon stuff or enhancements are required.

You'll have the best accomplishment with it in the event that you like to decide and explore different avenues regarding new food varieties and love to cook.

Be that as it may, following an alkaline diet will be intense for some individuals.

A ton of most loved food sources that are permitted with some restraint in different plans (counting lean meat, low-fat dairy, bread, and desserts) are illegal here. Protein is restricted to plant-based sources like beans and tofu. This implies you should ensure you get sufficient protein and calcium.

Eating out likewise can be a test. In the event that you travel a great deal for work or have a bustling timetable, you may feel impeded by all the food choice and prep.

At last, numerous alkaline diets neglect to address a main consideration in weight reduction and wellbeing achievement: work out. You ought to remember readiness for any good dieting plan that you pick. The American Heart Association and the CDC suggest getting at any rate 150 minutes of activity every week. In the event that you have any clinical issues or are rusty, converse with your primary care physician first.

1. Keralan hake curry

Prep:10 mins Cook:55 mins Serves 4

Ingredients:

- 1 tbsp groundnut oil
- 1 onion , finely cut
- little bundle coriander , leaves picked, follows finely chopped
- 1 thumb-sized piece ginger , stripped and cut into matchsticks
- 2 peppers (we utilized red and yellow)
- 2 tsp fenugreek seeds
- 2 tsp brown mustard seeds
- 200g cherry tomatoes
- 400g would coconut be able to drain

- 4 x 150g hake filets
- rice or naan, to serve

Technique:

1. Heat oven to 200C/180C fan/gas 6. Heat the oil in a shallow meal dish (or ovenproof skillet with a cover) over a medium heat. Add the onion, coriander stalks, ginger and peppers, and cook delicately with the cover on for 15 mins until relaxed and starting to brown. Turn up the heat, mix through the flavors and cook for 1 min more until sweet-smelling.

2. Tip in the tomatoes and pour in the coconut milk. Bring to an air pocket, at that point put in the oven with the top on for 20 mins. Eliminate from the oven and settle the hake on the sauce. Get back to the oven, revealed, for a further 10-15 mins or until the hake is cooked through. Season to taste, disperse with the coriander leaves and present with rice or naan to clean up the sauce.

2.   pigeon breast with spinach & bacon

Prep:5 mins Cook:15 mins Serves 2

Ingredients:

- 50g spread
- 100g smoked bacon lardons or chopped smoked bacon
- 2 cuts white sourdough
- 2 pigeon breasts
- 50g chestnut or wild mushrooms , cut
- 200g spinach
- 1 tbsp red wine or sherry vinegar

Strategy:

1. Heat a large portion of the spread in a large griddle, at that point fry the bacon for 5 mins

until beginning to fresh. Move to a plate using an opened spoon. Fry the bread in any extra bacon fat for 1 min on each side until fresh and brilliant, at that point move to a plate and put away.

2. Season the pigeon liberally with salt and pepper, and heat the leftover spread in the container until sizzling. Burn the pigeon for 2-3 mins on each side until brilliant, at that point move to a cleaving load up and leave to rest.

3. Return the seared bacon to the dish and turn up the heat. Dissipate over the mushrooms and fry for 3-4 mins until relaxed, at that point add the spinach, season and sprinkle in the vinegar. Turn the heat up to high and sautéed food until the spinach is shriveled. Split the spinach combination between the singed bread cuts. Finely cut the pigeon breasts, organize over the spinach and serve.

Works out in a good way For

Partridge in juice with apples and celery

Veal slashes with spinach and green pepper salsa

Pigeon pies with thistle sauce

3. Griddled chicken fajitas with squashed avocado

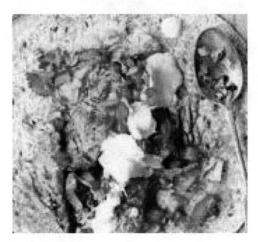

Prep:15 mins Cook:5 mins Serves 2

Ingredients:

- 2 garlic cloves , finely ground
- 150g pot plain bio yogurt
- ½ tsp smoked paprika
- ¼ tsp ground cumin
- ¼ tsp ground coriander
- ¼ tsp oregano
- 200g scaled down chicken bosom filets
- 2 tomatoes , chopped
- 1 little red onion , finely chopped
- 1 green stew , deseeded and finely chopped (optional)

- 4 tbsp chopped new coriander
- juice 1 lime
- 2 cultivated tortillas
- 1 avocado , divided and stoned

Technique:

1. Mix the garlic into the yogurt. Spoon 2 tbsp into a medium bowl, add the flavors and oregano, and mix well. Add the chicken and throw until covered.

2. Heat an iron dish and frying pan the chicken for 5 mins, turning once, until cooked entirely through yet clammy. (In the event that you need to sear the chicken, wipe a little oil in a non-stick container first or the flavors will consume.)

3. Blend the tomatoes in with the onion, stew (if using), coriander and lime to taste. Heat the tortillas adhering to pack guidelines. Scoop the substance from the avocado, squash half on top of every tortilla, at that point add the chicken and the salsa salad. Spoon over the garlicky yogurt, move up and eat while still hot.

Works out positively For

Chipotle hasselback yams

Mexican red rice

Mexican-style corn salad

4. South African chutney chicken

Prep:5 mins Cook:50 mins Serves 4

Ingredients:

- 1 tbsp olive oil
- 1 little onion, finely chopped
- 1 garlic clove, finely chopped
- 1 red stew, deseeded and finely chopped
- 6 tbsp mango chutney
- 1 tbsp Worcestershire sauce
- 6 tbsp mayonnaise
- 8 chicken thighs, skin on and bone in
- green serving of mixed greens, to serve
- 1 tbsp olive oil
- 1 little onion, finely chopped

- 1 garlic clove, finely chopped
- 1 red bean stew, deseeded and finely chopped
- 6 tbsp mango chutney
- 1 tbsp Worcestershire sauce
- 6 tbsp mayonnaise
- 8 chicken thighs, skin on and bone in
- green plate of mixed greens, to serve

Strategy:

1. Heat oven to 200C/180C fan/gas 6. Heat the oil in a skillet over a medium heat and cook the onion, garlic and stew for a couple of mins until mellowed. Mix in the chutney, Worcestershire sauce and mayonnaise. Taste and season.

2. Mastermind the chicken on a foil-lined heating plate and spoon over the chutney blend. Broil the chicken in the oven for 40-45 mins until cooked through and tacky. Present with a green plate of mixed greens.

3. Heat oven to 200C/180C fan/gas 6. Heat the oil in a skillet over a medium heat and cook the onion, garlic and bean stew for a couple of mins until relaxed. Mix in the chutney,

Worcestershire sauce and mayonnaise. Taste and season.

4. Mastermind the chicken on a foil-lined preparing plate and spoon over the chutney blend. Broil the chicken in the oven for 40-45 mins until cooked through and tacky. Present with a green plate of mixed greens.

5. Greenest coconut prawn noodles

Prep:10 mins Cook:10 mins Serves 2

Ingredients:

- 1 tbsp vegetable oil
- 2cm lump ginger , stripped and generally chopped
- 1 garlic clove , chopped
- 1 green bean stew , chopped
- ½ little pack coriander , stalks and leaves isolated, stalks chopped
- 130g (any or a blend of) spinach , rocket and watercress
- 400ml would coconut be able to drain
- 180g crude lord prawns

- 150g directly to wok noodles (we utilized rice noodles or utilize dried and cook for 2 mins not exactly the cooking time)
- ½ lime , squeezed

Strategy:

1. Heat the oil in large pot over a medium heat. Add the ginger, garlic, bean stew and coriander stalks and fry with a spot of salt until mellowed, around 3 mins. Add the greens and the majority of the coriander leaves, mix until withered, at that point tip the substance of the container into a blender with the coconut milk and 150-200ml water. Rush until smooth and radiant green. Or then again, on the off chance that you have a stick blender, use it to barrage every one of the ingredients in the dish.

2. Tip the sauce once more into the container, prepare and bring to the bubble. Add the prawns, noodles and the lime squeeze and cook for 4-6 mins until the prawns have become pink – at this point the noodles ought to be great. Spoon into two dishes and top with the excess coriander.

Works out in a good way For

Pork slashes with rhubarb and grains

Long-stem broccoli bread heat

Gnocchi with spice sauce

6. Braised ox cheek Wellingtons with peppercorn gravy

Prep:30 mins Cook:3 hrs and 45 mins Serves 2

Ingredients:

- 1 tbsp rapeseed, vegetable or sunflower oil
- 1 bull cheek , about 350g managed of any ligament
- 1 tbsp plain flour , in addition to a little for tidying
- 1 tsp English mustard powder
- 1 little red onion , generally chopped
- 3 thyme branches
- 1 hamburger stock solid shape
- 2 tbsp dried porcini mushrooms
- handle of margarine

- 1 garlic clove , squashed
- 100g chestnut mushrooms , finely chopped
- 500g pack puff baked good
- 4 cuts prosciutto
- 1 egg , beaten
- 100ml twofold cream
- 1 tsp dark peppercorns , squashed using a pestle and mortar
- cooked green vegetables , to serve

Technique:

1. Heat oven to 160C/140C fan/gas 3. Heat the oil in an ovenproof skillet (one with a tight-fitting cover) or flameproof meal dish over a high heat. Cut the bull cheek into 4 large pieces, at that point season well and throw in the flour and mustard powder. Spot the bits of meat in the hot oil – they should sizzle – and brown the meat all finished. Add the onion to the dish and keep cooking until mollified and beginning to caramelize. Add the thyme, stock 3D square, porcini and some flavoring. Empty 450ml water into the container, mixing to scratch any substantial pieces off the base.

Cover with a top and spot in the oven to cook for 3 hrs, turning the meat over in the fluid once while cooking, and fixing up with a sprinkle of water if the dish looks dry.

2. While the meat cooks, dissolve the margarine in a dish. Add the garlic, mix for 1 min yet don't brown, at that point add the mushrooms and cook for 10-12 mins until the dish is dry and the mushrooms are becoming brilliant. Season and put away.

3. At the point when their concocting time is, scoop the bull cheeks out of the fluid and utilize 2 forks to shred the meat – dispose of any pieces of fat or ligament. Strain the cooking fluid. Add 3-4 tbsp of the fluid back to the meat, alongside the cooked mushrooms. Cool, at that point cool the meat combination and the cooking fluid for 3 hrs, or up to 48 hrs.

4. Carry out the baked good on a floured surface to the thickness of a £1 coin. Remove 2 x 12cm circles and 2 x 15cm circles – utilize 2 plates to cut around on the off chance that you can. Orchestrate the prosciutto two by two on top of the more modest circles of cake, in a cross shape. Split the meat blend down the

middle and mount each bit on top of the prosciutto. Crease the prosciutto over the meat to encase it, at that point flip the little package of meat over, so the smooth side is looking up on top of the baked good. Brush the edge of every cake circle with a little beaten egg, at that point place the larger circles of baked good on top. Utilize your hands to make a domed focus, at that point pleat the edges with a fork (or your fingers) to seal in the meat. Score the baked good in a bungle design, at that point brush done with beaten egg.

5. Utilize any baked good pieces to remove a heart for every pie, leave this on top and brush with egg as well. Jab a steam opening on one or the other side of every heart. Spot every Wellington on a square of heating material and chill for at any rate 30 mins, or up to 24 hrs.

6. Heat oven to 200C/180C fan/gas 6 and put a preparing plate in the oven to heat up. Slide the Wellingtons on their material onto the hot plate and heat for 30 mins. In the interim, reheat the cooking fluid, add the cream and peppercorns, and keep warm until prepared to

eat. Serve every Wellington with green veg and the peppercorn sauce for pouring over.

Works out positively For

Raspberry and enthusiasm natural product martini

Salted caramel popcorn pots

Extreme onion rings with bacon mayo

7. Potato skin tacos

Prep:15 mins Cook:15 mins Serves 2

Ingredients:

- 2 heating potatoes
- 1 avocado , divided and cut
- ½ a red onion , finely cut
- 1 lime , squeezed
- 1 tbsp olive oil
- 75g cheddar , ground
- 2 tsp fajita zest blend
- 2 spring onions , finely cut
- ½ little pack coriander , leaves picked and follows finely chopped
- soured cream , to serve

Technique

1. Heat barbecue to high. Prick the potatoes with a fork and microwave on high for 5-10 mins until delicate. In the interim, throw the avocado and red onion with the lime juice and a large portion of the oil. When the potatoes have cooked, cut down the middle and scoop out the tissue into a bowl. Sprinkle the skins with the leftover olive oil and flame broil for 5-10 mins to fresh up.

2. Pound the potato with the cheddar, fajita zest blend, the vast majority of the spring onions and coriander stalks. When the potato skins have crisped up, eliminate from the flame broil and spoon the filling into them. Top with the coriander leaves, remaining spring onions and the soured cream, and present with the avocado and onion salad.

8.   Sweet potato, peanut butter & chilli quesadillas

Prep:15 mins Cook:45 mins Serves 2

Ingredients:

- 3 medium yams stripped and daintily cut
- 1 tbsp smoked paprika
- 3 tbsp olive oil , in addition to extra for brushing
- 1 additional large ready avocado
- ½ lime , zested and squeezed, in addition to wedges to serve
- 2 tbsp crunchy peanut butter
- 4 little flour tortillas
- sriracha stew sauce , to taste
- ½ little pack coriander , torn

Strategy:

1. Heat oven to 200C/180C fan/gas 6. Throw the yams with the paprika and 2 tbsp olive oil in a broiling tin. Cook for 15 mins, throwing partially through, until the potatoes are starting to fresh.

2. Stone, strip and hack the avocado, tip into a bowl with the lime squeeze and zing, and season liberally. Squash along with a fork and put away. In a little bowl, join the peanut butter and staying olive oil. Put away.

3. Heat a frying pan dish or griddle over a medium heat until hot. Brush every tortilla on one side with the leftover oil. Spot one tortilla, oiled-side down, in the skillet and spread over a large portion of the peanut butter combination, a large portion of the yams, a little stew sauce and a large portion of the coriander. Top with another tortilla, oiled-side up. Press down with a weighty pan and cook for 2-3 mins each side until the quesadilla is fresh outside and warm in the center. Rehash to make a subsequent quesadilla, at that point cut each into quarters and present with the squashed avocado and lime wedges.

Works out in a good way For

Incredible guacamole

Mexican potato wedges

Lighter nachos

9. Chipolatas in apple gravy with parsnip colcannon

Prep:20 mins Cook:40 mins Serves 4

Ingredients:

- 1 large potato , cut into lumps
- 4 parsnips , stripped and cut into lumps
- 8 chipolatas
- 50g margarine
- 2 large red apples , cored and cut into thin wedges
- 8 spring onions , cut, white and green parts isolated
- 1 tbsp flour
- 1 hamburger or chicken stock block
- 200g kale or Savoy cabbage, finely chopped
- 5ml milk

Technique:

1. Put the potato and parsnips in an extremely large container of water, bring to the bubble and stew for 10 mins or until the veg is delicate. In the mean time, cook the chipolatas in a large griddle. At the point when brown on all sides, move to a plate and add 25g margarine to the dish. Add the apples and white piece of the spring onions. Fry for 5-10 mins until mellowed and beginning to caramelize.

2. Add the kale to the bubbling veg for the last couple of mins, before the potatoes and parsnips are totally delicate. At the point when the kale has shriveled, channel the veg and leave to steam-dry in the colander. Heat the excess spread in a similar dish – don't stress over cleaning it out. Add the green pieces of the spring onions and sizzle for a couple of mins to relax.

3. Add the flour and stock solid shape to the apples and spring onions, mix for 1-2 mins, at that point add 400ml water, blending to a smooth sauce. Return the wieners to the dish

and air pocket in the sauce for a couple of mins until heated through. In the mean time, add the veg to the rich spring onions, alongside the milk and a lot of preparing, and crush until the potato and parsnips are smooth. Serve the colcannon with the chipolatas and the sauce spooned over the top.

Works out positively For

Caramelized carrots and onions

Broccoli with a crunch

10. Amarena cherry & almond tart

Prep:30 mins Cook:50 mins plus resting Makes 12 slices

Ingredients:

- 125g spread
- 125g brilliant caster sugar
- 225g plain flour
- ½ egg or 1 egg yolk
- For the frangipane filling
- 125g spread , at room temperature
- 125g brilliant caster sugar
- 3 medium eggs
- 1 lemon , zested
- 125g finely ground almonds or almond flour
- 120g Fabbri amarena cherries (see tip)
- icing sugar , for cleaning (optional)

Strategy:

1. Combine as one the margarine, sugar, flour, a spot of salt and the egg in a food processor to

make a mixture, at that point wrap and leave to rest in the ice chest for 30 mins. The batter ought to be cold yet simple to work with when you carry it out.

2. Then, make the frangipane filling. Soften the margarine in a container over a low heat, at that point put away to cool marginally. Beat the sugar with the eggs and lemon zing in a bowl until smooth. Pour in the softened spread while proceeding to beat, at that point add the ground almonds (or almond flour) and overlay into the combination. Heat oven to 175C/155C fan/gas 3½.

3. Line a buttered tart tin or ring mold (roughly 23cm) with the carried out cake batter, at that point trim any overhanging edges. Spread the frangipane equitably into the tin and organize the cherries on top with a portion of their syrup, so the highest point of the tart is shrouded in a meager layer.

4. Put the tart in the oven and prepare for around 40-45 mins until brilliant brown, puffed and firm to the touch. Leave to cool on a rack. Residue with some icing sugar, on the off chance that you like, prior to serving in cuts.

11. Brown butter linguine

Prep:5 mins Cook:15 mins Serves 1

Ingredients:

- 100g linguine (purchase all that can be expected)
- 25g spread
- ½ cut white bread , toasted and chopped into little pieces
- squeeze stew pieces
- 1-2 tbsp ground Grana Padano or veggie lover elective

Strategy:

1. Cook the pasta in salted bubbling water until still somewhat firm, at that point channel, saving a tad bit of the cooking water.
2. In the interim, cook a tad bit of the spread in a skillet until it froths at that point fry the bread until it is brilliant brown all finished. Tip into a bowl and crash the dish. Add the remainder of the margarine and heat it until it froths and

begins to brown. Add the stew pieces and a lot of dark pepper and cook for 1 min.

3. Tip the pasta back into the dish alongside a sprinkle of the cooking water and the cheddar and throw together altogether. Sprinkle on the seared bread and throw everything together once more.

Works out positively For

Chorizo hummus bowl

Pea and ham pot pie

Dhal with garam masala carrots

12. Fish finger wraps with cheat's tartare sauce

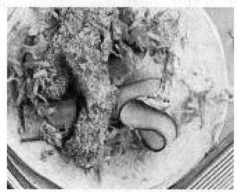

Prep:25 mins Cook:20 mins Serves 4
Ingredients:
- 100g linguine (purchase all that can be expected)
- 25g spread
- ½ cut white bread , toasted and chopped into little pieces
- squeeze stew pieces
- 1-2 tbsp ground Grana Padano or veggie lover elective

Strategy:
1. Cook the pasta in salted bubbling water until still somewhat firm, at that point channel, saving a tad bit of the cooking water.
2. In the interim, cook a tad bit of the spread in a skillet until it froths at that point fry the bread until it is brilliant brown all finished. Tip into a bowl and crash the dish. Add the remainder of the margarine and heat it until it froths and

begins to brown. Add the stew pieces and a lot of dark pepper and cook for 1 min.

3. Tip the pasta back into the dish alongside a sprinkle of the cooking water and the cheddar and throw together altogether. Sprinkle on the seared bread and throw everything together once more.

Works out positively For

Chorizo hummus bowl

Pea and ham pot pie

Dhal with garam masala carrots

13.   Spinach & nutmeg cannelloni

Prep:20 mins Cook:1 hr Serves 4 – 6

Ingredients:

- For the filling and fixing
- 500g pack prepared washed spinach
- 250g tub ricotta
- 250g tub mascarpone
- 140g ground parmesan (or veggie lover elective)
- 1 entire nutmeg
- 1 large egg
- 250g pack (6 large sheets) new egg lasagne
- For the pureed tomatoes
- 2 tbsp olive oil
- 3 large garlic cloves , finely chopped
- 500ml container passata
- 400g can chopped tomatoes
- 2 tbsp balsamic vinegar
- 1 tsp brilliant caster sugar
- little pack basil , generally chopped

Strategy:

1. Heat oven to 190C/170C fan/gas 5 in case you're serving straight away. Puncture the sack of spinach and cook in the microwave adhering to pack guidelines (in the event that you don't have a microwave, shrivel it in a dish with a scramble of olive oil). Leave to cool, press out as much fluid as possible, at that point finely slash.
2. In the interim, make the pureed tomatoes. Heat the oil and fry the garlic until mollified. Add the passata and tomatoes, vinegar and sugar, at that point season, cover and stew for 10 mins, blending every so often. Eliminate from the heat and add the basil. Tip into the foundation of a large, shallow preparing dish.
3. To make the filling, beat the ricotta and a fourth of the mascarpone with 50g of the Parmesan and the chopped spinach. Finely grind down the middle the nutmeg, at that point beat until very much blended. For the fixing, beat the excess mascarpone with the egg and another 50g of the Parmesan.
4. To make the cannelloni, partition the spinach filling into 6 sections, spoon a bit along the highest point of every lasagne sheet, at that point fold up into a major, fat cylinder. Slice down the middle across the center with a sharp blade so you have 2 more modest cylinders, at that point orchestrate on top of the pureed tomatoes. As you put them in the dish, push them marginally so the sauce overflows up the side of the cannelloni, as this will stop them remaining together when they are heated. Spoon the mascarpone blend on top, ensuring

you cover the pasta – in the event that it doesn't totally cover the sauce now, it will do once it softens and prepares. Disperse over the excess Parmesan and mesh over more nutmeg. In the case of making ahead, cover and chill – it will save for 1 day. Heat for 30-40 mins until brilliant and gurgling.

14. Keralan chicken coconut ishtu

Prep:20 mins Cook:1 hr and 20 mins Serves 4
Ingredients:

- 5 tbsp coconut oil or vegetable oil
- 5cm/2in cinnamon stick
- 6 green cardamom units
- 4 cloves
- 10 dark peppercorns , delicately squashed
- 1 star anise
- 15 curry leaves
- 1 medium onion , finely cut
- thumb-sized piece of ginger , stripped and finely chopped
- 6 garlic cloves , finely chopped
- 2-3 green chillies
- 2 tsp fennel seeds
- ½ tsp ground turmeric
- 1 tbsp ground coriander
- 600g chicken thighs , cleaned
- small bunch green beans , closes managed, divided if extremely long
- 400ml would coconut be able to drain
- 2 tbsp coconut cream
- 1 tsp vinegar (or to taste)

- large modest bunch child spinach , whitened and water pressed out
- little modest bunch new coriander , to embellish

Technique:
1. Heat the oil in a wide skillet (a karahi or wok is ideal), at that point add the cinnamon stick, cardamom units, cloves, peppercorns and star anise. When the seeds have quit popping, add the curry leaves and the onion and cook over a medium heat until clear. Add the ginger, garlic and green chillies, and sauté tenderly for 1-2 mins or until the garlic is cooked.
2. Granulate the fennel seeds to a fine powder in a zest processor or with a pestle and mortar, at that point add to the container with the turmeric, ground coriander and a spot of salt. Add a sprinkle of water and cook for 2 mins. Put the chicken in the skillet and cook in the flavor paste for 2 mins. Add water to come 33% of the path up the chicken, heat to the point of boiling, at that point decrease the heat and cook, covered, for 1 hr, mixing infrequently.
3. When the fluid has decreased, add the green beans and coconut milk (counting the flimsy milk that gathers at the lower part of the can), cover and cook for another 10 mins. Reveal and cook off the greater part of the abundance fluid, blending infrequently. Check the chicken is cooked completely through. Mix in the coconut cream, vinegar and spinach, and bring

to a stew. Taste and change the flavoring, and serve finished off with the coriander.

Formula TIPS

DID YOU KNOW?

This full-enhanced, velvety curry started with the Christians of Kerala. It is known as 'ishtu', or stew, as this is a combination of East and West.

15. Omelette pancakes with tomato & pepper sauce

Prep:10 mins Cook:20 mins Serves 2

Ingredients:

- 4 large eggs
- small bunch basil leaves
- For the sauce
- 2 tsp rapeseed oil , in addition to some extra for the flapjacks
- 1 yellow pepper , quartered, deseeded and daintily cut
- 2 garlic cloves , meagerly cut
- 1 tbsp juice vinegar
- 400g can chopped tomatoes
- wholemeal bread or salad leaves, to serve

Strategy:

1. First make the sauce. Heat the oil in a large griddle, and fry the pepper and garlic for 5 mins to mollify them. Spoon in the juice

vinegar and permit to sizzle away. Tip in the tomatoes, at that point measure in 33% of a container of water. Cover and leave to stew for 10-15 mins until the peppers are delicate and the sauce is thick.

2. In the mean time, make the hotcakes. Beat 1 egg with 1 tsp water and preparing, at that point heat a little non-leave skillet with a minuscule measure of oil. Add the egg combination and cook for 1-2 mins until set into a dainty flapjack. Lift onto a plate, cover with foil and rehash with different eggs. Move up onto warm plates, spoon over the sauce and disperse with the basil. Present with bread or a serving of mixed greens as an afterthought.

16. Lamb & garlic bread salad

Prep:20 mins Cook:35 mins Serves 4

Ingredients:

- little pack mint , finely chopped
- 2 tbsp additional virgin olive oil
- 1 lemon , zested and squeezed
- 8 sheep cutlets
- 1 cook-at-home garlic loaf (170g)
- 300g medium tomatoes , quartered
- 1 large cucumber , cut into large pieces
- little pack parsley , generally chopped
- 1 tsp nectar

Strategy:

1. Heat oven to 200C/180C fan/gas 6. Blend a large portion of the mint in with 1 tbsp oil, the lemon zing and a large spot of salt and dark pepper, at that point rub the combination everywhere on the sheep cutlets.

2. Heat the garlic bread for 15 mins, at that point permit to cool a bit. Attack pieces and get back to the oven for 5 mins to dry out.
3. Then, put a frying pan dish or large griddle over a high heat and, once hot, cook the sheep for 2-3 mins each side or until pleasantly singed outside yet at the same time pink in the center. (You may need to do this in two bunches.) Set to the side to rest while you make the plate of mixed greens.
4. Put the tomatoes and cucumber in similar hot dish and cook for 2 mins or until somewhat burned – you should do this in clusters. Tip into a large bowl and add the
5. toasted bread, staying mint and the parsley.
6. Blend the lemon squeeze in with the excess olive oil and the nectar, at that point season. Pour the dressing over the plate of mixed greens and throw tenderly so the tomatoes don't separate excessively. Serve the warm plate of mixed greens close by the sheep cutlets.

17. Green masala eggs

Prep:10 mins Cook:30 mins Serves 4
Ingredients:
- 6 eggs
- 350g brown basmati rice
- 2 tbsp rapeseed oil
- 1 onion , finely cut
- 2cm piece ginger , ground
- 1 tsp turmeric
- 1 tsp bean stew powder
- 1 tsp ground coriander
- 400ml would coconut be able to drain
- 2 green chillies , finely cut
- 1 tsp mango chutney
- little pack coriander

Technique:
1. Lower the eggs into a skillet of bubbling water and cook for 6 mins, at that point lift them out and cool under chilly running water. Cook the rice adhering to pack directions.
2. Heat a tad bit of the oil in a profound griddle and cook the onions until delicate. Add the

ginger and cook for 1 min, at that point mix in the turmeric, bean stew powder and coriander and cook for 1-2 mins or until fragrant. Add the coconut milk, the greater part of the chillies and the mango chutney, bring to a stew and cook for 5 mins.

3. Then, heat the remainder of the oil in a griddle or wok. Strip the eggs and mix them around in the hot oil until they brown and begin to air pocket and fresh all finished. Lift them cautiously out of the container and split them.

4. Generally slash the coriander and mix the majority of it into the masala with some salt. Add the eggs, disperse the remainder of the bean stew and coriander over the top and present with the rice.

18. Black bean, tofu & avocado rice bowl

Prep:20 mins Cook:25 mins Serves 4
Ingredients:

- 2 tbsp olive or rapeseed oil
- 1 red onion , chopped
- 3 garlic cloves , squashed
- 2 tsp ground cumin
- 2 x 400g jars dark beans , depleted and flushed
- zing 2 limes , at that point 1 squeezed, the other slice into wedges to serve
- 396g pack tofu , divided through the middle, at that point chopped into little pieces
- 2 tsp smoked paprika
- 2 x 200g pockets cooked brown rice
- 2 little ready avocados , divided, stoned, stripped and chopped
- little bundle coriander , leaves as it were
- 1 red bean stew , meagerly cut (optional)

Technique
1. Heat the barbecue to High. Heat 1 tbsp oil in a griddle, add the onion and cook, blending, for 5 mins or so until delicate. Add the garlic and sizzle for 30 secs more, at that point mix in the cumin and dark beans. Cook for 5 mins until the beans begin to pop and are hot through. Mix through the lime zing and squeeze, and season.
2. While the beans cook, put the tofu in a bowl and tenderly throw through the leftover oil, the paprika and some flavoring. Line a preparing plate with thwart and mastermind the tofu on top. Cook under the barbecue for 5 mins each side until burned all finished.
3. Heat the rice adhering to pack directions, at that point split between bowls. Top with the beans, tofu, avocado, coriander and a wedge of lime. Add a couple of cuts of bean stew as well, in the event that you like it zesty.

Formula TIPS

MAKE IT MEATY

Trade the tofu for some smoky pieces of chorizo – cut 50g per individual, eliminating the papery skin, and sizzle in a skillet until the juices run into the dish. In the event that your chorizo is hot, you might need to serve the dish with a mass of soured cream to temper the heat.

19. Plum & marzipan pie

Prep:50 mins Cook:30 mins - 50 mins plus chilling, cook time depends on the size of your pie Makes 1 large pie, about 25cm/10in (serves 6-8), 2 medium pies, about 18cm/7in each (serves 3-4) or 4 individual pies, about 10cm/4in each

Ingredients:

- For the cake
- 225g cold unsalted spread , chopped into little pieces
- 350g plain flour
- 50g icing sugar
- 1 large egg yolk (save the white for brushing the cake)
- For the filling
- 1kg plums (Victoria or Excalibar plums are delightful on the off chance that you can discover them), split, stoned, divided once more
- 100g brilliant caster sugar , in addition to extra for sprinkling
- 2 tsp cornflour
- 1 tbsp ground almonds or fine polenta

- 1 tsp almond remove
- 200g marzipan , chopped into 1.5cm solid shapes
- egg white , for brushing (saved from making the cake)
- cream or frozen yogurt, to serve

Strategy:
1. Put the spread and flour in a food processor with 1/4 tsp salt and mix until the combination looks like sodden breadcrumbs. Or then again do this by scouring the spread and flour together in a major bowl with your fingertips. Add the sugar and momentarily whizz again or mix to join.
2. Whisk the egg yolk with 2 tbsp cold water, and sprinkle over the flour combination. Utilize the beat catch to mix the blend again, continue to go until it begins to frame larger clusters. On the off chance that the combination appears to be excessively dry, add somewhat more water a tsp or 2 all at once, yet close to 3 tsp altogether.
3. Tip out onto a work surface and momentarily massage the batter to unite it into a smooth ball. Abstain from workaholic behavior or it will get extreme. Level the batter into a puck shape and envelop well by stick film. Chill for in any event 30 mins, or for as long as 2 days, or freeze for a very long time.
4. Tip the plums, sugar and cornflour into a large container, at that point throw to cover. Stew for 3-5 mins, blending from time to time, until the plums have recently started to relax. Tip

them into a sifter suspended over a large bowl, leave for 30 mins-1 hr, mixing each 10 mins, until the juice has all gathered in the bowl.

5. Eliminate the batter from the ice chest and separation into 2 pieces, one marginally larger than the other. Re-wrap the more modest piece of batter and put away. Gap the larger part of mixture into the quantity of pies you'd prefer to make, or leave entire for a large one. On a daintily floured surface, carry out the batter to the thickness of a 50p piece, or until sufficiently large to line the foundation of your pie plate or tin, with a little cake overhanging. Turn the batter over your moving pin, lift into the plate or tin and press it well into the corners. Disperse the almonds or polenta over the base.

6. Mix 2 tbsp of the stressed plum squeeze and the almond remove into the plums. Spoon the filling into the pie dish, dabbing the marzipan between the layers of plums as you go. Heat oven to 190C/170C fan/gas 5 and spot a preparing sheet on the center rack.
Top the pie with a cross section hull - follow the bit by bit pictures to perceive how to do this. In the first place, organize the cake strips on top of your pie, with space between every one. Overlay back substitute strips from the middle, at that point lay a strip across the center, close to the folds. Then, flip the collapsed strips back to cover the center baked good strip. Overlay back the strips that are woven under the center piece. At last, lay another strip across the center, and flip

substitute strips back once more. Rehash until you have a woven example.

7. Once covered, whisk the saved egg white and brush over the cake. Disperse with some additional sugar, at that point put on the preparing sheet and heat for 45 mins for a large pie, 35-40 mins for medium pies or 25-30 mins for smaller than expected pies, until brilliant and percolating. Cool for 10 mins prior to presenting with cream or frozen yogurt.

Formula TIPS

Adorn YOUR PIE

For tips, stunts and thoughts to style the top and sides of your pie, see our manual for 11 very simple approaches to adorn a pie.

Stay away from THE DREADED SOGGY BOTTOM

To ensure your pie has a fresh covering, utilize a metal or veneer pie plate, tin or a cake tin if your pie has a baked good base. Ensure the heating sheet is hot when the pie goes in the oven. Dissipate ground almonds or polenta over the base to absorb any additional juice from the natural product.

ADD A GLAZE

Whisk extra egg white from making the baked good with a fork until foamy and utilize this to coat the pie. On the off chance that you need the pie to have a pleasant brilliant shading, rush in a little caster sugar as well.

TOP TIPS

For this pie filling, I like to stew the natural product momentarily prior to preparing it in the pie to extricate the juice. Once sieved, I serve the juice as an afterthought – this prevents the base from going wet.

20. Spicy lamb with chickpeas

Cook:1 hr - 1 hr and 30 mins Serves 4
Ingredients:
- 700g cubed sheep
- 400g can tomatoes in rich juice
- 2-3 tsp harissa paste
- 410g can chickpeas , depleted
- modest bunch new coriander

Technique:
1. Flush the sheep and wipe off with kitchen paper. Tip into a large container and add tomatoes. Half fill the tomato can with water and add to the dish with the harissa paste and a decent sprinkling of salt and pepper.
2. Carry the fluid to the bubble, at that point diminish the heat, cover and stew for 1-11/4 hours, until the sheep is delicate. Wash the chickpeas and add them to the skillet, at that point stew for a further 5 minutes.
3. Taste and add really preparing if vital. Generally hack the coriander, at that point

dissipate over the dish. Present with couscous or rice.

21. Dhal with garam masala carrots

Prep:5 mins Cook:20 mins Serves 1

Ingredients:

- 75g red lentils
- 1 garlic clove , stripped
- handle of salted spread
- 2 carrots , cut into stick
- 1 tbsp rapeseed oil
- ½ tsp garam masala
- 1 tsp nigella seeds (kalonji, optional)
- 1 tsp Greek yogurt

Strategy:

1. Cook the lentils in 500ml water with the garlic clove for around 20 mins until the lentils are delicate. Fish the garlic clove out, smash it and mix it back into the lentils with the margarine. Season well. It ought to be spoonable like a thick soup – continue to stew if it's not thick enough.

2. Put the carrots in a dish, simply cover with water, bring to the bubble and stew until simply delicate, around 8-10 mins. Channel, at that point throw in the oil and garam masala. Tip into a griddle and fry until the carrots begin to brown, at that point add the nigella seeds, if using, and fry for another min.
3. Serve the dhal in a bowl with the yogurt and carrots, with the excess flavors and oil from the dish on top.

22. Persian basmati rice chelo (tahdig)

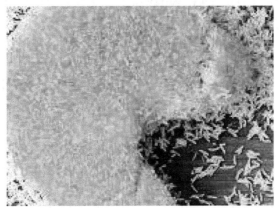

Prep:5 mins Cook:45 hrs - 1 hr and 30 mins
Serves 6
Ingredients:
- 500g basmati rice
- ocean salt drops
- light olive oil, for the skillet
- 60g margarine

Technique:
1. Heat a large pan over a medium heat if using gas, or a medium-high heat if using electric. Fill the container with bubbling water and add the rice with a liberal small bunch of squashed ocean salt chips. Bubble for 6–8 mins until the rice is parboiled. You will realize it is parboiled when the shade of the grains abandon the typical dullish white to a more splendid white, and the grains become somewhat stretched and start to relax.

2. Channel the rice and flush it quickly under chilly running water several minutes until it is cool. Line the lower part of the pan used to parboil the rice with some non-stick heating material (see tip).

3. Return the paper-lined pan to the hob and pour in a liberal shower of the oil with the margarine. Season the foundation of the container with some squashed ocean salt drops. Dissipate the rice into the container. Guarantee you dissipate it, don't pack it in – you need the daintiness of the falling rice to consider steam to ascend. Enclose the skillet top by a tea towel (to secure in the steam and make for a safe, tight seal), cover the container and cook the rice on the most minimal temperature workable for 45 mins if using gas, or a medium-low heat for 1 hr 30 mins if using electric. The grains ought to be puffed up when cooked.

4. When the rice is cooked, eliminate it from the container (it can assist with setting a large serving dish over the skillet and flip the rice onto the dish). Scratch out the tahdig (this is the hard piece, it signifies 'lower part of the container') and serve on top of the rice.

Formula TIPS

This formula has been lifted from Sabrina Ghayour's book Persiana.

Utilize BAKING PARCHMENT

Line the container with preparing material to forestall the tahdig from adhering to the base. In the event that you mess up or squash the paper prior to streamlining it again it makes it more flexible and simpler to utilize.

Works out in a good way For

Persian pilaf and simmered root portions

Persian sheep tagine

Persian pudding with whipped rose and nectar margarine

23. Mexican fiesta rice

Prep:15 mins Cook:25 mins Plus resting Serves 8

Ingredients:

- 2 tbsp olive oil
- 1 onion , finely chopped
- 2 peppers (pick your #1 shadings), finely chopped
- 4 garlic cloves , finely chopped or squashed
- 1 tsp cumin seeds or ½ tsp ground cumin
- 1 tbsp tomato purée
- little touch of sweet smoked paprika
- 250g basmati rice
- 450ml hot vegetable stock (ensure it's veggie lover cordial)
- finely chopped coriander and cut spring onions, to serve

Strategy:

1. Heat the oil in a large pan with a cover, at that point add the onion, pepper, garlic and cumin

and sizzle tenderly for 8-10 mins until the vegetables are delicate and brilliant. Mix in the tomato purée and smoked paprika and cook for 1 min, at that point mix in the rice.

2. Pour over the stock, at that point cover and bring to the bubble. Mix immediately, at that point cover again and place on the least heat conceivable. Stew for 10 mins. Mood killer the heat and leave, covered, for a further 10 mins. In the case of serving immediately, mix through the coriander and spring onions; then again, leave the rice to cool, chill, at that point re-fry prior to serving and mix the coriander and spring onions through toward the end.

24. Arroz al horno (baked rice)

Prep:20 mins Cook:55 mins Serves 8
Ingredients

- 2 tbsp additional virgin olive oil , in addition to extra to serve
- 800g thick pork gut pork cuts (around 8-10 cuts), split
- 150g dark pudding , generally chopped
- 100g stout bacon lardons
- 1 onion , finely chopped
- 2 red peppers , split, deseeded and cut
- 1 plum tomato , chopped
- 8 garlic cloves , generally chopped
- 4 tsp smoked paprika
- ¼-½ tsp dried stew pieces
- ½ x 400g can white beans , depleted (you can utilize haricot, spread beans or cannellini)
- 1.2l chicken stock
- 6 thyme or rosemary twigs
- 375g paella rice
- 1 lemon , squeezed (optional)

Strategy:
1. Heat oven to 200C/180C/gas 6. Heat a large portion of the oil in a profound fricasseeing or sauté container (or shallow meal dish) estimating around 30cm in measurement. Over a high heat, shading the pork gut cuts on each side in a few groups, at that point move to a bowl. Add the leftover oil to the dish and lower the heat to medium, at that point add the dark pudding and bacon and fry finished for a few mins. Eliminate with an opened spoon. Fry the onion and peppers for around 10 mins until delicate and pale gold, at that point add the tomato and cook until delicate. Add the garlic, smoked paprika and stew chips and cook for another 2 mins, at that point put the pork, dark pudding and bacon back in the skillet. Add the beans, stock and whichever spice you're using, and carry everything to the bubble.
2. Sprinkle the rice around the pork stomach, pushing it under the stock. Allow the stock to go to the bubble once more, season well, at that point move to the oven (leave it revealed). Cook for 20 mins without blending, at that point verify how the rice is getting along. The rice ought to be delicate and the stock ingested. In the event that it's not prepared, set back in the oven for another 5 mins, at that point check once more. Taste for preparing.
3. Press lemon juice over the top and shower over some additional virgin olive oil not long

prior to serving, on the off chance that you like.

25. Sushi rice

Prep:2 mins Cook:20 mins plus standing
Ingredients:
- 1 cup sushi rice (about 220g)
- sushi rice preparing, to taste (optional)

Technique:
1. The main thing to get right when cooking sushi rice is the proportion of rice to water. It's smarter to utilize a volume measure as opposed to gauging. Utilize a cook's 250ml estimating cup on the off chance that you have one, or a short glass, teacup or little mug. Whenever you've made one cluster, you'll know what amount cooked rice that action makes – it ought to be about 2½ cups.
2. Measure out 1 cup rice into a pan, wash the rice, whirling it around the container, at that point channel off the water. Make an effort not to lose any of the rice. Add 1½ cups water (about 375ml).
3. Carry the rice to a stew immediately, put on a tight-fitting cover and diminish the heat to low. Cook for 13 mins – don't take the top off.

4. Several grains at the top – the rice ought to be just about cooked and the water dissipated. If not, proceed to cook and check at 2 min stretches, each brand of rice will vary. Turn the heat off and leave the rice to remain with the cover on for 10 mins so all the dampness is ingested. Add sushi rice preparing, on the off chance that you like, and serve.

26. Crispy za'atar chicken pilaf with pomegranate

Prep:15 mins Cook:1 hr and 20 mins plus at least 1 hr chilling and resting Serves 4

Ingredients:

- 8 skin-on chicken thighs
- 3 tbsp olive oil
- 2 garlic cloves, squashed
- 1 lemon, squeezed
- 3 tbsp za'atar
- 70g pomegranate seeds
- ½ little bundle of parsley, finely chopped
- For the rice
- 1 tbsp olive oil
- 50g margarine
- 2 large onions, cut
- 220g basmati rice
- 350ml hot chicken stock
- 70g pistachios, chopped
- 1 tsp bean stew chips

Technique:

1. Throw together the chicken thighs oil, 1 tsp salt, garlic and lemon juice in a large bowl. Cover and chill for at any rate 1 hr, or up to 12 hrs.
2. Heat the oven to 180C/160C fan/gas 4, and heat a skillet over a high heat. Fry the chicken, skin-side down, for 5-7 mins, or until brilliant and fresh. Move to a heating plate and sprinkle with the za'atar, at that point broil for 10 mins.
3. For the rice, heat the oil and margarine in a large, shallow goulash or griddle over a low-medium heat. Fry the onions with a spot of salt for 15 mins until caramelized and tacky. Mix in the rice, stock, pistachios and stew chips. Season. Mastermind the cooked chicken thighs on top of the rice, and pour over any simmering juices from the plate. Cook in the oven for 45 mins, or until the rice is delicate. Eliminate from the oven, cover and rest for 5 mins.
4. Dissipate the chicken pilaf with the pomegranate seeds and parsley, at that point serve in shallow dishes.

Works out in a good way For

Beetroot rosti with green yogurt and smoked salmon

Burned onion and whipped feta flatbreads

Dim chocolate and energy natural product tart

27. West Indian spiced aubergine curry

Prep:30 mins Cook:15 mins Serves 2

Ingredients:
- 1 tsp ground cumin
- 1 tsp ground coriander
- ½ tsp ground turmeric
- 1 large aubergine
- 2 tbsp tomato purée
- ½ green bean stew , finely chopped
- 1cm piece ginger , stripped and finely chopped
- 2 tsp caster sugar
- ½-1 tbsp rapeseed oil
- 3 spring onions , chopped
- ½ bundle of coriander , shredded
- cooked rice , normal yogurt, roti and lime wedges, to serve

Technique:
1. Blend the dry flavors and 1 tsp salt together in a bowl and put away.

2. Cut the aubergine into 1cm rounds, at that point score the two sides of each round with the tip of a sharp blade. Rub with the flavor blend until very much covered (you should utilize the entirety of the blend), at that point move to a board. Put 150ml water in the unfilled flavor bowl with the tomato purée, bean stew, ginger and sugar. Put away.
3. Heat the oil in a large non-stick griddle over a medium heat and mastermind the aubergine in the skillet, covering the rounds if necessary. Fry for 5 mins on each side, or until brilliant. Add the fluid blend from the bowl, bring to a stew, cover and cook for 15-20 mins, turning the aubergine sporadically until it's cooked through. On the off chance that it appears to be dry, you may have to amount to 100ml more water to make it saucier. Season.
4. Dissipate over the spring onions and coriander, and present with rice, yogurt, roti and lime wedges for crushing over.

Formula TIPS

AUBERGINE and CHICKPEA CURRY

To loosen up extra aubergine curry, heat with a 400g can chickpeas, depleted, until warmed through. Dissipate with chopped coriander, on the off chance that you have any.

28. Rainbow rice paper rolls

Prep:40 mins No cook Makes 12
Ingredients:

- 50g fine vermicelli rice noodles
- 12 rice paper wraps
- modest bunch of mint or coriander leaves, or cut chives (or a blend)
- 200g cooked prawns , or cooked and shredded chicken
- ¼ cucumber , managed and finely cut into matchsticks
- 1 carrot , managed and finely cut into matchsticks
- 40g red cabbage , finely cut
- little modest bunch of radishes , managed and daintily cut
- ½ mango , stoned, divided and finely cut
- For the sesame plunging sauce
- 2 tbsp sweet bean stew sauce
- 1 tbsp tahini

- 1 tbsp low-salt soy sauce
- 1 tsp sesame oil , in addition to extra for sprinkling
- ½ lime , squeezed

Technique:

1. Absorb the noodles bubbling water from the pot, adhering to pack directions. Channel and wash under chilly running water to cool, at that point throw in a little sesame oil to stop them remaining together.
2. Then, make the plunging sauce by combining every one of the ingredients as one. Put away.
3. Fill a wide, shallow dish a couple of centimeters deep with warm water. Working with each rice paper envelop by turn, drench it for a couple of moments until it's adaptable, at that point lay it on a cleaving load up. Dissipate a portion of the spices down the middle, at that point top several prawns or a smidgen of chicken, at that point some veg pieces and mango, and a little heap of noodles. Attempt to keep the fillings in the middle, and don't overload. Fold the finishes of the fold around the ingredients to somewhat wall them in, at that point move up from the sides, keeping everything as close as possible. Put the completed moves on a plate covered with a soggy sheet of kitchen paper until you're done collecting every one of the rolls. Will keep in the refrigerator for up to 24 hrs. Present with the sesame plunging sauce.

29. Portuguese duck rice

Prep:30 mins Cook:1 hr and 45 mins plus cooling Serves 4 – 6
Ingredients:

- 1 entire duck , cut back of overabundance excess and jointed
- little pack coriander
- 2 inlet leaves
- 1 thyme twig
- 1 star anise
- 1 leek (green top just, save the white part for the rice)
- 1 onion , split
- 1 carrot
- 1 large orange , zested and squeezed
- For the rice
- 2 tbsp olive oil
- saved white piece of the leek
- 1 onion , cut
- 1 garlic clove
- 250g basmati rice
- 100g chorizo , cubed

- mint or coriander leaves, to serve
- salad , to serve (optional)

Strategy:

1. Put the duck in your largest container, cover with water and add the coriander, straight, thyme, star anise, leek top, onion, carrot, orange zing and a granulating of dark pepper. Spot over a medium heat and bring to the bubble, skimming off any filth from the surface. Turn down the heat marginally, cover and stew for 45 mins, at that point turn off the heat and let the duck cool in the stock for 15 mins. Channel the stock from the duck, saving it to cook the rice. Leave the duck to rest until adequately cool to deal with, at that point shred the meat away from the bone.

2. Heat oven to 180C/160C fan/gas 4. To make the rice, heat the oil in a large skillet over a medium-high heat and sauté the leek, onion and garlic for 10-12 mins or until delicate and fragrant. Add the rice and fry for 5 mins or until the grains are becoming brilliant and fresh, and adhering to the container. Add 400ml of the duck stock and cook for 15 mins, covered, without mixing, or until the rice is puffed and dry.

3. Mix the duck meat and squeezed orange through the rice, season, at that point move the blend to an oiled broiling tin or meal dish. Top with the chorizo and spot on a high rack in the oven to cook for 20-25 mins or until the rice is fresh and brilliant. Topping with coriander or mint leaves, and present with a

serving of mixed greens, in the event that you
like.

30. Honey, sesame & orange king prawns

Prep:10 mins Cook:10 mins Serves 4

Ingredients:
- 2 tsp sesame oil
- 1 large orange , zested and squeezed
- 3 tbsp nectar
- 2 tbsp low-salt soy sauce
- 1 tbsp rice vinegar
- 3 tbsp cornflour
- 2 tbsp sesame seeds
- liberal touch of Chinese five-flavor powder
- 300g crude lord prawns
- 3 tbsp sunflower or vegetable oil
- 1 garlic clove , daintily cut
- 2 spring onions , cut
- 200g long-grain rice , cooked, to serve

Strategy:
1. Blend the oil, orange zing and juice, nectar, soy and vinegar in a bowl, at that point consolidate the cornflour, sesame seeds, five-

zest and a touch of salt in another bowl. Run a little blade down the rear of each prawn, so they butterfly out as they cook, assisting more with saucing stick to them.

2. Throw the prawns through the cornflour combination. Heat the oil in a large wok or griddle. At the point when it's exceptionally hot, add the garlic. Sizzle for 10 secs, however don't allow it to brown. Add the prawns and any flour and seeds left in the bowl. Sautéed food over a high heat for a couple of moments, until the prawns are pink and the sesame seeds are brilliant. Tip the prawns onto a plate and empty the sauce blend into the wok. Air pocket for a couple of moments until thickened. Add the prawns back to the wok and mix to cover in the sauce. Heat through for an additional 30 seconds. Top with spring onions and present with rice.

Formula TIPS

USING SOY SAUCE

We have utilized low-salt soy sauce in our recipes to decrease the salt substance, however you may like to utilize more modest sums than proposed to remain inside the suggested day by day admissions.

Conclusion

I would like to thank you for choosing this book It contains recipes which are easy to prepare and contain more health benefits. Hope you will enjoy cooking these dishes. Do prepare for yourself and enjoy.

THE ESSENTIAL ALKALINE RECIPES FOR BEGINNERS

Table of Contents

INTRODUCTION

Here are 4 Life-Changing Benefits of Following an Alkaline Diet:

Battles against Fatigue: Too much corrosive in the body diminishes the stockpile of oxygen. This declines the cell's capacity fix and gather supplements. On the off chance that you feel lethargic and tired for the duration of the day, even with the appropriate measure of rest, this could be the pointless development of corrosive.

Reinforces Immune System: Unbalance in pH lessens the body's capacity to battle microscopic organisms and infections. Without the oxygen, microorganisms and infections can flourish the most in the circulatory system. Alkalizing is a need to kill the likelihood of sickness.

Diminishes aggravation: Over-acridity in the body can build irritation, when you have coronary illness, joint pain, or malignant growth your framework is in a fiery state. An eating regimen that comprises of alkaline-framing food varieties holds aggravation under wraps.

Reinforces Bone: As individuals age, the body normally goes through calcium from our bones Calcium in a vital factor in adjusting the blood and body pH. Without the calcium, our bones become weak, prompting osteoporosis.

What is an Alkaline Diet and how would I begin? An Alkaline eating routine permits us to put food varieties on a scale to characterize them as either corrosive shaping or alkaline-framing. By and large food sources with a pH level of 1-7 are considered acidic, or the meats, dairy and espresso we referenced before. Food varieties between 7-14 are considered alkaline and end up being supplement thick and cell reinforcement rich. Extraordinary instances of solid, alkaline food sources include: citrus organic products (esp. new lemon), vegetables and crude, natural nuts like almonds. Our's bodies will probably discover an equilibrium in the alkaline zone between 7.35 - 7.45 pH - to accomplish this a general guideline is to follow a 80/20 eating regimen with the goal that your day by day feast comprises principally of organic products and vegetables and less of meats and dairy (and espresso!).

31. Lamb dopiaza with broccoli rice

Prep:20 mins Cook:1 hr and 30 mins Serves 2

Ingredients:

- 225g sheep leg steaks , cut back of overabundance excess and cut into 2.5cm/1in pieces
- 50g full-fat characteristic bio yogurt , in addition to 4 tbsp to serve
- 1 tbsp medium curry powder
- 2 tsp cold-squeezed rapeseed oil
- 2 medium onions , 1 meagerly cut, 1 cut into 5 wedges

- 2 garlic cloves , stripped and finely cut
- 1 tbsp ginger , stripped and finely chopped
- 1 little red bean stew , finely chopped (deseeded in the event that you don't care for it excessively hot)
- 200g tomatoes , generally chopped
- 50g dried split red lentils , washed
- 1/2 little pack of coriander , generally chopped, in addition to extra to decorate
- 100g pack child leaf spinach
- For the broccoli rice
- 100g wholegrain brown rice
- 100g little broccoli florets

Technique:

1. Put the sheep in a large bowl and season well with ground dark pepper. Add the yogurt and 1/2 tbsp of the curry powder, and mix well to consolidate.

2. Heat a large portion of the oil in a large non-stick pot. Fry the onion wedges over a high heat for 4-5 mins or until gently browned and simply delicate. Tip onto a plate, put away and return the dish to the heat.

3. Add the excess oil, the cut onions, garlic, ginger and stew, cover and cook for 10 mins or until delicate, blending at times. Eliminate the top, increment the heat and cook for 2-3 mins more or until the onions are touched with brown – this will add loads of flavor, however ensure they don't get scorched.

4. Diminish the heat again and mix in the tomatoes and remaining curry powder. Cook for 1 min, at that point mix the sheep and yogurt into the skillet and cook over a medium-high heat for 4-5 mins, mixing routinely.

5. Empty 300ml virus water into the container, mix in the lentils and coriander, cover with a top and leave to cook over a low heat for 45 mins – the sauce ought to stew delicately and you can add a sprinkle of water if the curry gets somewhat dry. Eliminate the top each 10-15 mins and mix the curry.

6. With 30 minutes of the curry cooking time remaining, cook the rice in a lot of bubbling water for 25 mins or until simply delicate. Add the broccoli florets and cook for a further 3 mins. Channel well.

7. Eliminate the top from the curry, add the held onion wedges and keep on stewing over a high heat for a further 15 mins or until the sheep is delicate, blending consistently. Not long prior to serving, mix in the spinach, a modest bunch at a time, and let it shrivel. Present with the yogurt, coriander and broccoli rice.

Formula TIPS

Putting away LEFTOVERS

Freeze the cooked and cooled curry in sealable sacks or a cooler verification holder for as long as 2 months. Defrost for the time being in the cooler and reheat in a pan until steaming hot all through.

Works out positively For

Red pepper hummus with crispbread snaps

Yam dhal with curried vegetables

32. Lamb biryani

Prep:10 mins Cook:50 mins Plus at least 2 hrs marinating and resting Serves 6

Ingredients:

- 400g sheep neck, cut into little solid shapes
- 4 garlic cloves, ground
- 1 tbsp finely ground ginger
- 1 tbsp sunflower oil
- 1 large onion, chopped
- 1 tbsp cumin seeds
- 1 tbsp nigella seeds
- 1 tbsp Madras flavor paste
- 200g basmati rice, washed well
- 8 curry leaves
- 400ml great quality sheep or chicken stock

- 100g paneer, chopped
- 200g spinach, cooked and water pressed out
- To serve
- chopped coriander
- cut green chillies
- plain yogurt

Strategy:

1. Throw the sheep in a bowl with the garlic, ginger and a large touch of salt. Marinate in the cooler short-term or for at any a few hours.

2. Heat the oil in a meal. Fry the sheep for 5-10 mins until beginning to brown. Add the onion, cumin seeds and nigella seeds, and cook for 5 mins until beginning to mollify. Mix in the curry paste, at that point cook for 1 min more. Dissipate in the rice and curry leaves, at that point pour over the stock and bring to the bubble. Then, heat oven to 180C/160C fan/gas 4.

3. Mix in the paneer, spinach and some flavoring. Cover the dish with a tight top of foil, at that point put the top on to guarantee it's all

around fixed. Cook in the oven for 20 mins, at that point leave to stand, covered, for 10 mins. Carry the dish to the table, eliminate the top and foil, disperse with the coriander and chillies and present with yogurt as an afterthought.

33. Wild mushroom & ricotta rice with rosemary & thyme

Prep:10 mins Cook:45 mins Serves 2

Ingredients:

- 15g dried porcini mushrooms
- 1 tbsp balsamic vinegar
- 1 tbsp vegetable bouillon powder
- 1 tbsp rapeseed oil
- 1 large onion , finely chopped
- 200g pack little catch mushrooms
- 1 tbsp new thyme leaves
- 1 tsp chopped rosemary
- 3 garlic cloves , cut
- 170g brown basmati rice
- 2 leeks , washed and cut
- 50g ricotta

- 15g vegan Italian-style hard cheddar , finely ground
- parsley , to serve

Techniqu:

1. Put the dried mushrooms in an estimating container and pour over 800ml bubbling water. Mix in the balsamic and bouillon. Leave to drench.
2. Heat the oil in a large wok or griddle and fry the onion for 8 mins until delicate and brilliant. Add the catch mushrooms, thyme, rosemary, garlic and dark pepper, at that point cook, mixing at times, for 5 mins. Pour in the dried mushrooms and fluid, at that point mix in the rice and leeks.
3. Cover and leave to stew for 30 mins until the fluid has been ingested and the rice is delicate yet nutty. Eliminate from the heat, at that point mix in the ricotta and ground cheddar, and serve dissipated with parsley leaves.

34. Sticky chicken drumsticks & sesame rice salad

Prep:10 mins Cook:30 mins Serves 2

Ingredients:

- 4 chicken drumsticks
- 2 tbsp clear nectar , in addition to 1tsp
- 2 tbsp tamari (or soy sauce if not gluten free)
- 3 tbsp vegetable oil
- 2 tbsp sesame oil
- 120g basmati rice
- 70g kale , chopped
- juice 2 limes
- 100g radishes , divided
- 1 tbsp sesame seeds

Technique:

1. Heat oven to 200C/180C fan/gas 6. Put the drumsticks in a simmering tin. Blend 2 tbsp nectar, the tamari, 1 tbsp veg oil and 1 tbsp sesame oil in a bowl, at that point pour over the chicken – ensure each piece is covered. Cook for 25-30 mins.

2. Then, cover the rice with 240ml water and bring to the bubble. Cook for 8-10 mins until delicate. Back rub the kale with 1 tbsp veg oil for 5 mins until relaxing (this makes it less chewy). Sprinkle over the lime juice, remaining sesame oil and nectar, and season. Add the radishes and put away.

3. Fry the rice in the leftover veg oil in a non-stick container to dry out. Add to the kale, and throw to join.

4. Serve the drumsticks with the plate of mixed greens and dissipate over the sesame seeds.

Works out in a good way For

Minty summer rice salad

Crunchy green beans with radishes

Sesame barbecued asparagus pontoons

35. Thai broccoli rice

Prep:25 mins Cook:10 mins serves 4 (or 6 as a side)

Ingredients:

- 100g salted peanuts
- 1 head of broccoli , cut into florets and the stem cut down the middle
- 2 tbsp olive oil
- 1 red onion , finely diced
- 1 garlic clove , squashed
- 1 tbsp ground ginger
- 1 medium red stew , deseeded and finely diced
- ½ little red cabbage , shredded
- 1 red pepper , deseeded and cut into strips
- little pack coriander , generally chopped
- For the dressing

- zing and juice 1 lime
- 2 tbsp tamari
- ½ tbsp brilliant caster sugar
- 2 tbsp olive oil

Strategy:

1. Heat a skillet over a medium heat and add the peanuts. Toast equally, consistently shaking the dish, at that point eliminate and put away. Put the broccoli in a food processor and heartbeat until it would seem that green couscous grains. Void into a large bowl and put away.

2. Heat the oil in a large skillet and fry the onion, garlic, ginger and stew until delicate and fragrant. Add the broccoli rice to the skillet and blend through, ensuring everything is very much covered. Sauté for 3-4 mins until still somewhat firm. Move to a large bowl and add the red cabbage, red pepper, a large portion of the coriander and a large portion of the toasted peanuts. Blend to consolidate.

3. To make the dressing, whisk the lime zing and juice, tamari, sugar and oil together until

joined. Throw the dressing through the broccoli rice and move to a serving bowl or individual dishes. To serve, decorate with the leftover coriander and peanuts.

36. Smoky spiced Jollof rice & coconut-fried plantain

Prep:10 mins Cook:40 mins Serves 6

Ingredients:

- 400g basmati rice
- 400g can plum tomatoes
- 1 red pepper
- 1 red onion , divided
- 1 garlic clove
- 1 scotch cap bean stew (deseeded on the off chance that you don't care for it excessively hot)
- 4 tbsp vegetable oil or sunflower oil
- 3 straight leaves
- 1 thyme branch

- 1 tsp cayenne pepper
- 1 tsp smoked paprika
- 1 tsp ground cumin
- 1 tsp ground dark pepper
- 60g tomato purée
- For the singed plantain
- 4 tbsp coconut oil
- 2 plantains , stripped and cut into 1cm rounds

Technique:

1. Put the rice in a sifter, wash completely to eliminate the starch, at that point absorb clean virus water for 5 mins. Channel and standard heat up the rice for 5 mins until practically cooked, at that point channel, wash and put away.
2. Mix the tomatoes, pepper, a large portion of the red onion, the garlic and bean stew until smooth.
3. Finely cut the excess onion half. Heat the vegetable oil in a large, high-sided container. Add the cut onion, narrows and thyme, and cook on a medium heat for 8 mins until the onion is softened and sweet-smelling.

4. Add the flavors with 1 tsp ocean salt, cook for a couple of mins more, at that point add the tomato purée and cook for 1-2 mins.

5. Add a large portion of the tomato and pepper blend (freeze the rest for sometime later). Add the semi-cooked rice and blend completely to cover with the sauce. Add somewhat more water, turn down the heat, mix and cover with a top for 5-10 mins until cooked through. Cooking time will rely upon the kind of rice, so continue to check it. Try not to stress in the event that it gets on the base, this will add to the flavor. Season to taste and eliminate the cove leaves prior to serving.

6. To cook the plantain, basically heat the coconut oil in a high-sided container until hot. Fry the plantain, turning sometimes, for a couple of mins until delicate and brilliant. Present with the rice.

37. Roast cauliflower with prosciutto & taleggio

Prep:10 mins Cook:30 mins Serves 2-4

Ingredients:

- 1 large cauliflower
- olive oil , for brushing
- 125g taleggio cheddar , cut
- 4 cuts prosciutto
- 4 liberal tbsp crème fraîche
- 75g gruyère , ground
- rocket or watercress, delicately dressed, to serve (optional)

Strategy:

1. Heat oven to 220C/200C fan/gas 7. Eliminate the leaves from the cauliflower and cut out the base (without removing such a lot of that the head breakdowns). Slice the cauliflower down the middle, at that point into four cuts – two from every half – that are about 2cm thick. Put these on a heating sheet, brush done with oil and season with pepper (no salt). Cover the preparing sheet firmly with foil and cook for 12 mins.

2. Eliminate from the oven, remove the foil and turn the heat down to 200C/180C fan/gas 6. Set the sheet back and cook for 8 mins. Eliminate from the oven – the pieces ought to be brilliant on one side – and turn the cauliflower over. Put a portion of the taleggio, a cut of prosciutto and a spoonful of crème fraîche on every cauliflower piece. Sprinkle with the gruyère, at that point get back to the oven.

3. Cook for another 8 mins, or until the cauliflower is brilliant and the cheddar has dissolved. The cauliflower pieces ought to be totally delicate. Serve straight away with the

rocket or watercress, on the off chance that you like.

Works out positively For

Broccoli and cauliflower cheddar

Southern-style macintosh 'n' cheddar

Cauliflower steaks with broiled red pepper and olive salsa

38. Skinny lamb biriyani

Prep:15 mins Cook:20 mins Serves 2

Ingredients:

- For the cauliflower pilau
- 350g cauliflower florets
- ½ tsp turmeric
- 3 cardamom units , daintily squashed
- ½ tsp fennel seeds , daintily squashed
- a couple of portions of dark onion seeds or nigella seeds
- For the zesty sheep
- 1 tbsp rapeseed oil
- 1 large onion , finely chopped
- 1 tbsp finely chopped ginger
- 1 red bean stew , deseeded and finely chopped
- 2 garlic cloves , daintily cut
- 1 tsp ground cumin

- 1 tsp ground coriander
- 200g exceptionally lean sheep steak, cut into scaled down pieces
- 200g can chopped tomatoes
- 1 tsp bouillon
- 15g toasted chipped almonds
- 50g pomegranate seeds
- modest bunch little mint leaves

Technique:

1. Put the cauliflower in a food processor and heartbeat until it is diminished to rice-sized pieces. Tip into a large bowl and mix in the turmeric, cardamom, fennel seeds, dark onion seeds and some flavoring. Cover with stick film, puncture and put away.

2. For the zesty sheep, heat the oil in a non-stick wok and fry the onion and ginger for 10 mins until delicate and brilliant. Add the stew and garlic, and cook for 1 min more.

3. Mix in the cumin and coriander, cook momentarily, at that point throw in the sheep and pan fried food for 1-2 mins until pale brown. Add the tomatoes and the bouillon, and

cook for 2 mins - you are focusing on a thick sauce and truly delicate sheep that is still somewhat pink and delicious.

4. Then, put the cauliflower in the microwave and cook on high for 3 mins. Tip out onto serving plates, dab the sheep and sauce in patches over the rice, at that point dissipate with the almonds, pomegranate seeds and mint leaves to serve.

39. Lighter cauliflower cheese

Prep:20 mins Cook:30 mins Serves 4

Ingredients:

- 400ml semi-skimmed milk
- 2 tbsp cornflour
- 2 garlic cloves
- 1 large cauliflower , about 1kg, untrimmed
- 75g extra-develop cheddar , coarsely ground
- 25g parmesan , coarsely ground
- 1 tbsp clipped chives
- 1½ tsp Dijon mustard
- 150ml buttermilk

Technique:

1. Blend 2 tbsp of the milk with the cornflour and put away. Press the garlic cloves in a garlic smasher to crush – yet not pound – them. Put them in a container with the remainder of the milk and heat until simply going to the bubble. Quickly eliminate from the heat and leave to implant.

2. Trim any leaves from the cauliflower and cut out the thick principle tail, at that point cut the cauliflower into florets. Carry a large container of water to the bubble. Add the cauliflower, get back to the bubble, at that point stew for around 5 mins until just cooked yet with a touch of nibble.

3. Heat oven to 200C/180C fan/gas 6. Tip the cauliflower into a large colander, channel well, at that point move to a shallow ovenproof dish, about 1.5 liters (see tip, left). Combine the two cheeses as one. Mix 2 loaded tbsp with the chives and a pounding of pepper, and save for sprinkling over.

4. Mix the cornflour blend into the warm milk. Return the container to the heat and bring to the bubble, blending, until thickened and smooth. Eliminate from the heat, dispose of

the garlic, at that point mix in the cheddar until it has softened. Mix in the mustard and buttermilk, and season with pepper. Pour the sauce over the cauliflower to equally cover, at that point sprinkle over the held cheddar blend. Heat for around 25 mins or until rising round the sides and brilliant on top.

40. Vegan nuggets

Prep:20 mins Cook:40 mins plus 1 hr chilling
MAKES 30

Ingredients:

- 300g cauliflower florets (or 3/4 little cauliflower)
- 2 carrots , chopped (about 165g)
- ½ medium onion , chopped
- 1 tbsp olive oil
- 1 garlic clove , squashed
- 2 tbsp nourishing yeast
- 2 tsp yeast remove
- 400g can cannellini beans , depleted
- 50g gram (chickpea) flour
- olive oil , for the heating plate
- For the covering

- 100g gram flour , in addition to some extra
- 100g breadcrumbs (use sans gluten if vital)

Technique:

1. Heartbeat the cauliflower, carrots and onion in a food processor until finely chopped, similar to rice. Heat the oil in a large griddle and tenderly fry the blend for 12-15 mins until softened. Add the garlic and fry for a further 1 min, at that point remove the heat and mix in the healthful yeast and yeast extricate. Put away.

2. Mix the beans into a soft purée in a food processor, at that point add to the veggie blend and consolidate well. Mix in the flour and season. Put in the cooler to solidify for 1 hr.

3. Heat the oven to 220C/200C fan/gas 7. Line a large heating plate with preparing material and coat with a little olive oil. To make the covering, blend the gram flour with 150ml water using a fork so it takes after beaten egg, at that point season. Dissipate the additional gram flour on a plate and fill a second with the breadcrumbs.

4. Fold the bean combination into pecan estimated pieces, at that point smooth to frame chunk shapes. Dunk the pieces first in the gram flour, at that point in the gram hitter, lastly move in the breadcrumbs – handle cautiously as they will be somewhat delicate. At the point when the chunks are completely covered, spread them out on the readied plate.
5. Heat for 20 mins, at that point use utensils to turn every piece over and prepare for a further 15 mins until they are dim brilliant and fresh. Leave to cool for 20 mins prior to presenting with your decision of plunging sauces.

41. Courgette & cauliflower yellow curry

Prep:10 mins Cook:30 mins Serves 4

Ingredients:

- 2 tbsp vegetable oil
- 2 little onions , finely chopped
- 2 garlic cloves , squashed
- 2 tbsp yellow curry paste
- 400ml would coconut be able to drain
- 450g cauliflower florets
- 2 large courgettes , divided and cut
- 250g basmati rice
- 1 red bean stew , deseeded and cut
- little pack coriander , leaves as it were

Technique:

1. Heat the oil in a large, profound griddle and cook the onions for 5 mins until delicate, yet not browning. Add the squashed garlic and yellow curry paste and mix for a further 2 mins.
2. Pour in the coconut milk, add a large portion of a jar of water (using the coconut milk can), and bring to a delicate stew. When stewing, add the cauliflower and courgette. Cover and stew for 10 mins, at that point eliminate the top and keep cooking until the sauce decreases and thickens a bit. Season well.
3. Then, cook the rice adhering to pack directions. Serve in shallow dishes with the curry, finished off with the stew and a dissipating of coriander.

Works out positively For

Cauliflower rice

Coconut rice

Pea, feta and quinoa spring moves with broil tomato nam prik

42. Beef & lentil cottage pie with cauliflower & potato topping

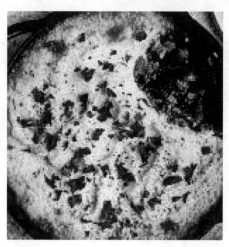

Prep:20 mins Cook:1 hr and 20 mins Serves 4

Ingredients:

- 1 tbsp olive oil
- 250g minced meat
- 1 large carrot , coarsely ground
- 1 tbsp tomato purée
- 200g red lentil
- 600ml meat stock
- 140g frozen pea
- 1 ¼kg potato , cubed
- 1 large cauliflower (about 400g), cut into florets
- 150ml milk

- 50g spread
- 100g develop cheddar , ground

Strategy:

1. Heat oven to 200C/180C fan/gas 4. Heat the oil in a large dish and add the minced meat. Cook for 5 mins until browned all finished, at that point add the carrot and cook for 2 mins more.

2. Mix in the tomato purée and add preparing. Cook for a couple of mins, at that point add the lentils and stock. Stew for 20 mins, at that point mix in the peas.

3. In the interim, carry a container of water to the bubble and add the potatoes. Stew for 15 mins, at that point add the cauliflower and stew for a further 10 mins until the veg is delicate.

4. Channel, at that point return the veg to the search for gold few mins to dry out. add the milk, margarine and preparing, and pound together. At last, add the cheddar, holding a modest bunch, and blend well. Cover and set to the side 500g of the squash blend for the

frankfurter formula tomorrow (see 'works out positively for', right).

5. Spoon the mince into a large simmering dish, around 30 x 20cm, and spoon the squash over the top. Sprinkle with cheddar and heat until brilliant, around 30 mins.

43. Lentil lasagna

Prep:15 mins Cook:1 hr and 15 mins Serves 4

Ingredients:

- 1 tbsp olive oil
- 1 onion , chopped
- 1 carrot , chopped
- 1 celery stick, chopped
- 1 garlic clove , squashed
- 2 x 400g jars lentils , depleted, washed
- 1 tbsp cornflour
- 400g can chopped tomato
- 1 tsp mushroom ketchup
- 1 tsp chopped oregano (or 1 tsp dried)
- 1 tsp vegetable stock powder
- 2 cauliflower heads, broken into florets
- 2 tbsp unsweetened soya milk

- touch of newly ground nutmeg
- 9 dried without egg lasagne sheets

Strategy:

1. Heat the oil in a container, add the onion, carrot and celery, and tenderly cook for 10-15 mins until delicate. Add the garlic, cook for a couple of mins, at that point mix in the lentils and cornflour.

2. Add the tomatoes in addition to a canful of water, the mushroom ketchup, oregano, stock powder and some flavoring. Stew for 15 mins, mixing every so often.

3. In the interim, cook the cauliflower in a dish of bubbling water for 10 mins or until delicate. Channel, at that point purée with the soya milk using a hand blender or food processor. Season well and add the nutmeg.

4. Heat oven to 180C/160C fan/gas 4. Spread 33% of the lentil blend over the foundation of an earthenware preparing dish, around 20 x 30cm. Cover with a solitary layer of lasagne, snapping the sheets to fit. Add another third of the lentil blend, at that point spread 33% of

the cauliflower purée on top, trailed by a layer of pasta. Top with the last third of lentils and lasagna, trailed by the leftover purée.

5. Cover freely with thwart and prepare for 35-45 mins, eliminating the foil for the last 10 mins of cooking.

44. Marinated lamb leg, romanesco & pickled walnuts

Prep:30 minsCook:30 minsplus overnight marinating Serves 6

Ingredients:

- 1.2kg sheep back end or boneless leg, parceled into equivalent pieces
- 500g live normal yogurt
- little pack rosemary , leaves and stalks isolated
- 2 entire romanesco , leaves eliminated
- 3 tbsp vegetable oil
- 7 salted pecans , 4 finely chopped and 3 split for serving, in addition to 1 tbsp pickling fluid
- 60ml olive oil

- 500ml new sheep stock

Strategy:

1. The prior night, cut back the excess from the sheep at that point blend in with the yogurt and rosemary leaves. Cover and put in the ice chest to marinate for the time being.

2. The following day, trim the tail off a romanesco so it sits upstanding on a board. Cut 5cm off each side with a bread blade (keep these off-slices to make the couscous). Cut the remainder of the romanesco into three thick cuts. Rehash with the other romanesco. Oil a large, non-leave preparing plate with 1 tbsp vegetable oil. Lay the romanesco cuts in a solitary layer and sprinkle with somewhat more vegetable oil. Season with salt and dissipate over the rosemary stalks, prepared to broil.

3. Finely slash or heartbeat the romanesco off-cuts in a food processor until they are the surface of couscous. Blend the finely chopped pecans into the couscous with the olive oil, and season with salt.

4. Heat oven to 200C/180C fan/gas 6. Wipe the marinade off the sheep and season with ocean salt. Heat 2 tbsp vegetable oil a large ovenproof skillet. Fry the sheep until brilliant all finished, at that point broil in the oven for 8-12 mins, contingent upon how uncommon you like it. Put the romanesco in the oven simultaneously. When the sheep is prepared, eliminate from the oven, flip the romanesco cuts over so they roast on the two sides, and cook for a further 10 mins. Cover and rest the sheep in the search for gold mins.
5. In the interim, stew the stock in a wide pan with 1 tbsp of the pecan pickling vinegar from the container for 10 mins until it frames a jus.
6. Cut the sheep and present with the romanesco cuts, some couscous, a large portion of a pecan and the jus.

45. Cauliflower & cheese fritters with warm pepper relish

Prep:30 mins Cook:1 hr and 20 mins Serves 5

Ingredients:

- For the squanders
- 1 cauliflower - you need 350g/12oz
- 100 g/4 oz plain flour
- 4 eggs , beaten
- 100 g/4 oz feta cheddar , generally disintegrated into little lumps
- 125g ball mozzarella , attacked little pieces
- zing 1 lemon , in addition to wedges to serve
- little pack level leaf parsley , generally chopped
- olive oil , for fricasseeing
- For the relish

- 1 onion , chopped
- 2 red peppers , chopped
- little piece ginger , finely ground
- 2 garlic cloves , squashed
- 1 red stew , chopped (leave the seeds in)
- 1 tbsp olive oil
- 2 tsp yellow mustard seed
- 250 g/9 oz tomatoes , generally chopped assuming large, left entire if cherry
- 50 g/2 oz delicate light brown sugar
- 50 ml/2 fl oz red wine vinegar
- 2 tbsp sultana

Strategy:

1. For the relish, mellow the onion, peppers, ginger, garlic and stew in the oil in a large pot. Once softened, add the mustard seeds, tomatoes, sugar and vinegar. Cover and stew for 30 mins, at that point uncover and stew for 10 mins more until delicate and tacky as opposed to excessively sassy. Mood killer the heat and mix in the sultanas. This relish will keep in the refrigerator for as long as 3 days, or freeze for as long as a month.

2. Heat up a large pot of water. Quarter the cauliflower and remove the majority of the focal large tail. Weigh 350g cauliflower for the formula and put the rest in the cooler to utilize some other time. Generally cleave the cauliflower – you should wind up with a blend of little florets and some better pieces. When the water is bubbling, add all the cauliflower, cover and cook for 3 mins precisely. Promptly channel, at that point tip everything back into the pan and set back over a low heat, to dry out for a couple of mins.

3. Put the flour into a large bowl with a lot of preparing and bit by bit race in the eggs to make a smooth hitter. Mix in the cheeses, lemon zing and the majority of the parsley, at that point tenderly mix in the entirety of the cauliflower.

4. Pop your oven on low so you can keep the wastes warm while you cook in clusters. Spot an old tough oven plate (anything unstable may clasp) or a durable skillet or iron straight onto the grill. Wipe with some olive oil, at that point spoon on some combination to make approximately 10-12cm round wastes. Fry for

3-5 mins until brilliant under and the player simply looks set on the top, at that point utilize a fish cut to flip the squanders over and push down with the rear of the cut to crush any large cauliflower bits and smooth the bottoms a piece. Cook again for 3-5 mins until brilliant, at that point move to a material lined plate and keep warm in the oven while you cook the rest.

5. To serve, warm up the relish somewhat, disperse the squanders with outstanding parsley and add some lemon wedges.

Works out in a good way For

Grilled sheep with sweet mint dressing

46. Charred spring onion & olive rice salad

Prep:15 mins Cook:15 mins Serves 8 as a side

Ingredients:

- 100g pitted Spanish green olives , depleted
- bundle spring onions (150g)
- 1 tsp olive oil
- 750g cooked blended grains and rice (or 3 x 250g pockets)
- 3 tbsp sherry or red wine vinegar
- 100g sundried tomatoes , cut
- 50g chipped almonds , toasted
- 2 celery sticks, chopped
- 50g manchego shavings or vegan elective (optional)

Technique:

1. String the olives onto metal or bamboo sticks. Heat an iron container or light the grill, at that point when the flares have subsided and the coals are white, throw the spring onions with the oil and barbecue for 8-10 mins to cook until delicate. Barbecue the olives for a couple of mins, turning routinely, until they look somewhat singed. Eliminate the spring onions from the barbecue and cut into reduced down pieces. Eliminate the olive sticks from the flame broil.

2. Heat the grains and rice pockets, if using, in the microwave for 2 mins until warm. Throw with the vinegar, some flavoring and the sundried tomatoes with a little sprinkle of the oil from the container. Leave for a couple of mins for the dressing to be retained.

3. Throw the olives, spring onions, toasted almonds and celery into the rice. To serve, mix through the manchego, if using, and season to taste.

Formula TIPS

COOKING WITH OLIVES

Burning olives makes them juicier just as giving incredible surface and profundity of flavor.

KEEP IT VEGAN

To guarantee the plate of mixed greens is veggie lover, use juice vinegar (or check the mark on the red wine or sherry vinegar), preclude the manchego and top with extra chipped almonds or entire toasted almonds, generally chopped. You can likewise add 4 tbsp raisins, for pleasantness, on the off chance that you like.

47. Jerk chicken with rice & peas

Prep:25 mins Cook:45 mins

Plusovernightmarinating Serves 6

Ingredients:

- 12 chicken thighs, bone in
- 1 lime, divided
- hot sauce, to serve (optional)
- For the marinade
- 1 major bundle spring onions, generally chopped
- thumb-sized piece ginger, generally chopped
- 3 garlic cloves
- ½ a little onion
- 3 scotch cap chillies, deseeded in the event that you need less heat
- ½ tsp dried thyme, or 1 tbsp thyme leaves
- 1 lime, squeezed

- 2 tbsp soy sauce
- 2 tbsp vegetable oil
- 3 tbsp brown sugar
- 1 tbsp ground allspice
- For the rice and peas
- 200g basmati rice
- 400g would coconut be able to drain
- 1 bundle spring onions, cut
- 2 large thyme branches
- 2 garlic cloves, finely chopped
- 1 tsp ground allspice
- 2 x 410g jars kidney beans, depleted

Technique:

1. To make the jerk marinade, consolidate the spring onions, ginger, garlic, onion, scotch hat chillies, dried thyme, lime juice, soy sauce, vegetable oil, brown sugar and ground allspice in a food processor alongside 1 tsp salt, and mix to a purée. In case you're experiencing difficulty getting it to mix, simply continue killing the blender, mixing the combination, and attempting once more. At last it will begin

to mix up – don't be enticed to add water, as you need a thick paste.

2. Taste the jerk combination for preparing – it should taste pretty pungent, however not terribly, puckering pungent. You would now be able to toss in more chillies if it's not zesty enough for you. On the off chance that it tastes excessively pungent and harsh, have a go at including a touch more brown sugar until the combination tastes even.

3. Make a couple of cuts in 12 chicken thighs and pour the marinade over the meat, scouring it into every one of the hole. Cover and leave to marinate for the time being in the ice chest.

4. On the off chance that you need to grill your chicken, get the coals consuming 1 hr or so before you're prepared to cook. Valid snapped meats are not by and large flame broiled as we consider barbecuing, however kind of smoke-barbecued. To get a more valid jerk insight, add some wood chips to your grill, and cook your chicken over lethargic, circuitous heat for 30 mins.

5. To cook in the oven, heat to 180C/160C fan/gas 4. Put the chicken pieces in a broiling

tin with the divided lime and cook for 45 mins until delicate and cooked through.

6. While the chicken is cooking, set up the rice and peas. Wash the basmati rice in a lot of cold water, at that point tip it into a large pot. Add the coconut milk, spring onions, thyme twigs, garlic and ground allspice.

7. Season with salt, add 300ml virus water and set over a high heat. When the rice starts to bubble, turn it down to a medium heat, cover and cook for 10 mins. Add the kidney beans to the rice, at that point cover with a top. Leave off the heat for 5 mins until all the fluid is ingested.

8. Crush the broiled lime over the chicken and present with the rice and peas, and some hot sauce on the off chance that you like it truly hot.

48. Chicken mole with coriander rice

Prep:30 mins Cook:2 hrs Serves 6

Ingredients:

- 2 ancho chillies
- 2 tbsp sunflower oil
- 8 bone-in chicken thighs , skins eliminated
- 2 onions , chopped
- 2 tsp ground cumin
- 1 ½ tsp cinnamon
- 3 garlic cloves , generally chopped
- 50g raisin
- 2 tbsp smooth peanut butter
- 2 tbsp chipotle paste
- 400g can chopped tomato

- 25g dim chocolate (search for one with at any rate 70% cocoa solids)
- 1 little red onion , cut into rings
- juice 1 lime , in addition to wedges to serve (optional)
- 150ml pot soured cream
- For the coriander rice
- 600g long grain rice
- large pack coriander , finely chopped
- zing 2 limes and squeeze of 1

Technique:

1. Put the chillies in a bowl and add sufficient bubbling water to simply cover. Leave to mellow for 20 mins. In the event that you can't discover anchos, flame broil red peppers until they're truly darkened and delicate. Cool them, at that point strip and use depending on the situation in the formula, adding 1 tsp smoked paprika and some additional chipotle to re-make the sweet, smoky flavor.

2. In the interim, heat the oil in a flameproof meal dish, season the chicken, at that point brown on all sides. You may need to do this in

bunches so you don't stuff the dish. Eliminate to a plate. Add the onions to the dish and cook for 5 mins until softened. Add the flavors and cook for 1 min until fragrant.

3. Eliminate the chillies from their splashing fluid, holding the fluid, and dispose of the stalks and seeds. Put in a food processor with 4 tbsp of the drenching fluid, the garlic and raisins. Whizz to a paste, at that point tip into the dish. Add the peanut butter, chipotle paste, tomatoes and 400ml water (top off the tomato can and twirl to get all the tomato bits out). Return the chicken to the dish and season. Cover with a top and stew, blending sporadically, for 1 hr.

4. Eliminate the chicken pieces to a plate. Using 2 forks, shred the meat and dispose of the bones. Return the chicken to the sauce, add the chocolate and keep cooking, revealed, for 30 mins more. In the event that the sauce resembles it's getting excessively thick, add a portion of the bean stew dousing fluid or some water.

5. Cook the rice adhering to pack guidelines. In the interim, put the red onion in a little bowl.

Add the lime juice and a touch of salt. Leave to pickle until prepared to serve. At the point when the rice is cooked, add the coriander and lime zing and squeeze, and cushion up with a fork. Eliminate the mole from the heat, disperse with the salted red onion and serve close by the rice, with soured cream and lime wedges, in the event that you like.

Formula TIPS

Stew KNOW-HOW

Ancho is the name given to the dried poblano pepper, which is filled in South America and utilized in its dried structure to season sauces and stews. Ancho chillies are large, with dim brown or dark skins and a sweet, raisin-like flavor. They have a medium zest.

49. Beef rendang & turmeric rice

Prep:40 mins Cook:2 hrs and 30 mins Serves 6

Ingredients:

- 3 tbsp vegetable oil
- 2kg hamburger shin or skirt, cut into reduced down 3D shapes
- 2 lemongrass stalks, slammed (see 'Tip' for how to plan)
- 2 x 400ml jars coconut milk
- 4 tbsp parched coconut
- 2 kaffir lime leaves, torn
- 1 ½ tbsp chicken stock powder (we utilized one from an Asian general store)
- 2 tbsp tamarind paste
- 1 tsp brilliant caster sugar
- ¼ tsp salt

- For the paste
- 15 dry chillies
- 6-8 child shallots
- thumb-sized piece ginger, chopped
- thumb-sized piece galangal, stripped and chopped (utilize ginger in the event that you can't discover it)
- 3 lemongrass stalks, chopped
- For the rice
- 2 tbsp oil
- 2 tsp mustard seeds
- 2 tsp turmeric
- 10 curry leaves (optional)
- 700g jasmine rice
- 2 tsp chicken stock powder

Technique:

1. For the paste, absorb the chillies bubbling water for 15 mins. Channel, eliminate seeds and whizz with the remainder of the paste ingredients in a little food processor until smooth.

2. Heat the oil in a wok or a weighty based flameproof goulash dish. Fry the paste for 5

mins until the fragrance is delivered. Add the meat and the lemongrass, and blend well. When the hamburger begins to lose its pinkness, add the coconut milk and 250ml water. Bring to the bubble, at that point lower to a stew, uncovered. Mix infrequently to abstain from staying, and all the more frequently towards the end.

3. In the mean time, toast the coconut in a griddle on a low heat for 5-7 mins until brilliant brown. Put away to cool. Using a blender, coarsely mix it to better pieces – yet not very fine. Put aside.

4. After 2 hrs, add the coconut, kaffir lime leaves, chicken stock powder, tamarind paste, sugar and salt to the container. Stew for 30 mins more. You should begin to see the oil isolating from the blend. It's prepared when the meat is delicate and practically self-destructing.

5. For the rice, utilize a substantial based pot with a cover. Heat the oil in the dish and add the mustard seeds. When the seeds begin popping, add the turmeric, curry leaves (if using) and rice, and blend well. Add the chicken stock and 1 liter of water. Bring to the bubble, at that

point go down to the least stew and cook, covered, for 5 mins. Eliminate from the heat, with the cover on and leave to steam for 25 mins.

Formula TIPS

Planning LEMONGRASS

Strip off the main layer and utilize the base, less sinewy part just, disposing of the top 5cm. Any extras freeze well.

50. Pollo en pepitoria

Prep:35 mins Cook:1 hr and 10 mins Serves 4

Ingredients:

- great touch of saffron
- 4 tbsp additional virgin olive oil
- 6 garlic cloves
- 35g whitened almonds
- 30g flat bread , torn
- 2 tbsp parsley , chopped, in addition to extra to serve
- 8 skin-on and bone-in chicken thighs
- 1 onion , finely chopped
- 1 carrot , chopped
- 1 celery stick, chopped
- 250ml dry sherry

- 350ml chicken stock
- 1 cinnamon stick , broken in two
- touch of ground cloves
- 2 sound leaves
- 2 eggs , hard-bubbled, shelled and split
- 2 tbsp chipped almonds , toasted

Strategy:

1. Put the saffron in a little bowl with 75ml of just-bubbled water. Mix and put away. Heat 2 tbsp of the oil in an expansive, shallow goulash dish. Cook the garlic until pale gold in shading, at that point add the whitened almonds and bread, and keep on singing until everything is brilliant. Tip into a food processor with some salt and pepper and the parsley, and whizz together.

2. Heat 2 more tbsp of the oil in the container and brown the chicken all finished, preparing as you cook. Put in a bowl and put away.

3. Eliminate everything except around 2 tbsp of chicken fat from the container and cook the onion, carrot and celery until brilliant. Add the sherry, blending to remove any brown pieces

that have adhered to the skillet. Pour in the stock and the saffron (with its water), and bring to the bubble, at that point turn the heat down to a stew. Add the flavors and straight leaves, and set the chicken back in the skillet with any juices. Season and tenderly cook the chicken for around 40 mins with the top on.

4. Move the chicken to a bowl once more, leaving the sauce in the skillet, and cover with foil to keep warm. Eliminate the yolks from the eggs and generally slash the whites. Pound the egg yolks in a little bowl and continuously blend a few tbsp of the sauce. Carry the leftover sauce to the bubble to decrease a messed with (you need it to simply cover the chicken), at that point turn the heat down. Eliminate the inlet and cinnamon stick. Add the egg yolks and cook for a couple of mins until the blend has thickened. Mix in the almond combination that you made before (this will thicken the sauce, as well). Set the chicken back in the container and heat it for around 3 mins, spooning the sauce over it. Season to taste.

5. Disperse over the additional parsley, the almonds pieces and the chopped egg whites (in

case you will utilize them). You can serve this directly from the dish with some rice, in the event that you like.

51. Spicy nduja arancini

Prep:35 mins Cook:1 hr Makes 20

Ingredients:

- 2 tbsp olive oil
- 1/2 onion, finely chopped
- 1 large garlic clove, squashed
- 1/2 tsp fennel seeds, squashed
- 300g risotto rice
- 400g can chopped tomatoes
- 800ml hot chicken stock
- 80g parmesan, finely ground
- 50g nduja hotdog, finely chopped
- 150g mozzarella, cut into 3D shapes
- 100g plain flour
- 3 medium eggs, beaten
- 200g panko breadcrumbs

- vegetable oil, for profound searing

Strategy:

1. Heat the olive oil in a goulash dish over a low heat, and fry the onion with a touch of salt for 10-12 mins, or until softened. Add the garlic and fennel seeds, and cook for 1 min more. Mix in the rice and cook

2. Pour in the tomatoes and a large portion of the stock, and turn the heat to medium-high. Cook, mixing persistently, until the stock is totally vanished. Add the excess stock, a spoon at a time, adding more when the past option is consumed by the rice. Cook until the rice is still somewhat firm, around 15-20 mins.

3. Mix in the parmesan and nduja, at that point spread the risotto out over a preparing plate and leave to cool to room temperature.

4. Scoop the cooled risotto into 20 even segments, marginally larger than a golf ball. Smooth one of the balls into a circle in your grasp, put a piece of mozzarella in the middle, at that point encase with the rice. Fold into a

ball. Rehash with the leftover risotto and mozzarella.

5. Tip the flour, eggs and panko breadcrumbs into three separate shallow dishes. Roll every risotto ball in the flour, at that point the egg, lastly the breadcrumbs. Move the balls to a heating plate. Half-fill a large, hefty based pot with vegetable oil and heat over a medium-low heat to 170C, or until a slice of bread becomes brilliant in the oil inside 45 seconds. Cautiously lower the risotto balls into the oil in clumps, and fry each bunch for 8-10 mins, or until brilliant brown and gooey in the middle. Channel on a plate fixed with kitchen paper.

Formula tip

To freeze, make the formula up to the furthest limit of stage 3, at that point pack the risotto balls into a large food sack and freeze. Thaw out altogether in the ice chest short-term before profound fricasseeing.

52. Creamy tomato risotto

Prep:5 mins Cook:35 mins Serves 4

Ingredients:

- 400g can chopped tomato
- 1l vegetable stock
- handle of spread
- 1 tbsp olive oil
- 1 onion, finely chopped
- 2 garlic cloves, finely chopped
- 1 rosemary twig, finely chopped
- 250g risotto rice
- 300g cherry tomato, split
- little pack basil, generally torn
- 4 tbsp ground parmesan

Technique:

1. Tip the chopped tomatoes and a large portion of the stock into a food processor and heartbeat until smooth. Fill a pan with the excess stock, bring to a delicate stew and keep over a low heat.

2. Then, place the margarine and oil in the foundation of a large pan and heat delicately until the spread has dissolved. Add the onion and delicately cook for 6-8 mins until softened. Mix in the garlic and rosemary, at that point cook for 1 min more. Add the rice and cook, blending, for 1 min.

3. Begin adding the hot stock and tomato combination about a quarter at a time. Allow the risotto to cook, blending regularly, adding more stock as it is retained. After you have added a large portion of the stock, add the cherry tomatoes. After 20-25 mins, the rice ought to be smooth and delicate, the cherry tomatoes softened and the entirety of the stock ought to be spent.

4. Cover and leave for 1 min, at that point mix in the basil. Serve sprinkled with Parmesan and a decent pounding of dark pepper.

53. Arancini balls

Prep:40 mins Cook:1 hr and 5 mins Makes 18
Ingredients:
- 2 tbsp olive oil
- 15g unsalted margarine
- 1 onion, finely chopped
- 1 large garlic clove, squashed
- 350g risotto rice
- 150ml dry white wine
- 1.2l hot chicken or veg stock
- 150g parmesan, finely ground
- 1 lemon, finely zested
- 150g ball mozzarella, chopped into 18 little pieces
- vegetable oil, for profound searing
- For the covering
- 150g plain flour
- 3 large eggs, softly beaten
- 150g fine dried breadcrumbs (panko functions admirably)

Technique:

1. Heat the oil and margarine in a pan until frothy. Add the onion and a touch of salt and fry tenderly over a low heat for 15 mins, or until softened and clear. Add the garlic and cook for another min. Mix in the rice and cook for a further min, at that point pour in the wine. Bring to the bubble and cook until the fluid is diminished significantly. Pour into equal parts the stock and stew, blending ceaselessly, until the vast majority of the fluid is retained. Add the leftover stock a ladleful at a time as the rice ingests the fluid, blending, until the rice is cooked through (this should take around 20-25 mins). Mix in the parmesan and lemon and season to taste. Spread the risotto out into a lipped plate and leave to cool to room temperature.

2. Scoop the cooled risotto into 18 equivalent segments – they ought to be somewhat larger than a golf ball. Level a risotto ball in your grasp and put a piece of the mozzarella in the middle, at that point encase the cheddar in the rice and fold it into a ball. Rehash with the leftover risotto balls.

3. Put the flour, eggs and breadcrumbs into three separate shallow dishes. Dunk each readied risotto ball into the flour, trailed by the eggs lastly, the breadcrumbs. Move to a plate and put away.

4. Half-fill a large, hefty based pot with vegetable oil and heat over medium-low until it peruses 170C on a cooking thermometer or until a slice of bread becomes brilliant brown in the oil

inside 45 seconds. Lower the risotto balls into the oil in clusters and cook for 8-10 mins, or until brilliant brown and softened in the middle. Put away on a plate fixed with a spotless kitchen towel.

5. Eat the arancini warm, or present with a fundamental pureed tomatoes for plunging.

Formula TIPS

ROLLING THE ARANCINI

Utilize somewhat wet hands to fold the risotto into balls – this will help shape the arancini, and stay away from any dilemmas.

54. Fragrant pork & rice one-pot

Prep:15 mins Cook:30 mins Serves 4

Ingredients:

- 4-6 great quality hotdogs
- 1 tbsp olive oil
- ½ onion , finely chopped
- 2 garlic cloves , squashed
- 2 tsp each ground cumin and coriander
- 140g long grain rice
- 850ml vegetable stock
- 400g can chopped tomato
- ½ little pack coriander , leaves picked

Strategy:

1. Split the hotdog skins, press out the meat, at that point fold it into little meatballs about the size of a large olive. Heat the oil in a large non-stick pan, at that point brown the meatballs well on all sides until cooked – you may have to do this in clumps. Put the meatballs away.

2. Add the onion and garlic to the container. Relax for 5 mins, mix in the flavors and rice, at that point cook for another min. Pour in the stock and tomatoes. Bring to a stew, scraping up any sausagey bits from the lower part of the skillet. Stew for 10 mins until the rice is simply cooked, at that point mix in the meatballs with some flavoring. Scoop into bowls, dissipate with coriander and present with dry bread.

Formula TIPS

TIP

The most straightforward approach to roll a meatball is with somewhat wet hands – it will stop the blend adhering to your fingers.

MAKE IT WITH PASTA

Italian pork balls with spaghetti: Brown the frankfurter meatballs in a griddle until brilliant, at that point put away. Relax the onion and garlic as above, at that point mix in 1 tsp dried oregano, the chopped tomatoes, ½ can water and 1 tsp sugar. Stew until sassy, at that point mix in the meatballs for a couple of mins until cooked through. Serve over spaghetti, finished off with ground Parmesan.

Works out in a good way For

Caramel apple disintegrate

55. Tamarind aubergine with black rice, mint & feta

Prep:25 mins Cook:40 mins Serves 4
Ingredients:

- 2 large aubergines
- 4 tsp tamarind paste
- 2 tsp sesame oil
- 1 red stew , deseeded and daintily cut
- 1 tbsp sesame seeds
- 200g dark rice
- 6 spring onions , finely cut
- 100g feta , disintegrated
- 2 little packs mint , generally chopped
- little pack coriander , generally chopped, holding a couple of leaves, to serve
- zing 1 large lime
- For the dressing
- 2 tbsp dull soy sauce
- juice 1 lime
- 5cm/2in piece ginger , stripped and finely ground (juices what not)

- touch of sugar

Strategy:
1. Heat oven to 200C/180C fan/gas 6. Slice the aubergines down the middle lengthways and, with the tip of a blade, score the tissue profoundly in a mismatch precious stone example – however don't penetrate the skin. Push on the edges of the parts to open the cuts. In a little bowl, consolidate the tamarind paste and sesame oil. Brush the combination over the aubergine, driving it into the cuts. Spot on a heating plate, sprinkle over the bean stew and sesame seeds, at that point broil, cut-side up, for 25-35 mins or until the tissue is truly delicate.
2. Put the rice in a little strainer and wash under running water for 1 min until the water runs clear. Tip the rice into a little pan and add 650ml virus water. Bring to the bubble, decrease the heat and stew for around 35 mins until the rice is delicate. Channel under chilly running water.
3. Make the dressing by whisking every one of the ingredients along with a spot of salt. Change the flavoring to taste, adding somewhat more sugar, salt or lime juice, in the event that you like.
4. In a major bowl, combine as one the dark rice, spring onions, feta, mint, chopped coriander, and the lime zing and dressing. Sprinkle the saved coriander leaves over the aubergine parts and present with the rice.

56. Mauritian chicken curry

Prep:20 mins Cook:30 mins Serves 4
Ingredients:
- 2 tbsp vegetable oil
- 8 curry leaves , finely chopped
- 1 medium onion , finely chopped
- 2 garlic cloves , finely ground
- 2cm ginger , finely ground
- 1 cinnamon stick
- 1 green stew , finely chopped
- 1 tbsp thyme leaves
- 3 tbsp Mauritian curry powder
- 600g skinless chicken thigh filets, chopped
- 2 medium tomatoes , chopped
- 2 large potatoes , cut into quarters
- ½ red onion , finely cut, to serve
- 1 tbsp coriander leaves , to serve
- basmati rice , cut cucumber, new rotis and satini pomme d'amour, to serve
- For the satini pomme d'amour
- 2 large ready tomatoes , finely chopped
- 1 green stew , finely chopped

- ½ white onion , finely chopped
- 1 tbsp olive oil

Strategy:
1. Heat the oil in a large pot over a low-medium heat. Drop in the curry leaves, onion, garlic, ginger, cinnamon stick, stew and thyme and cook for 5 mins until the onion has softened, mixing routinely to forestall adhering to the skillet.
2. Blend the curry powder with a sprinkle of water in a bowl to make a runny paste. Add the paste to the dish and give it a decent mix until fragrant, around 30 seconds. Keeping the heat on a low-medium stew with the goal that the flavors don't consume, add the chicken pieces and mix to cover in the curry.
3. Add the chopped tomatoes, potatoes and 1 tsp salt. Pour in water to simply underneath the level of the chicken and potatoes. Cook for around 25 mins until the potatoes and chicken are cooked through, at that point dispose of the cinnamon stick.
4. To make the satini pomme d'amour, combine every one of the ingredients as one in a bowl. Spoon the curry into bowls and dissipate over the coriander leaves and red onion. Present with fleecy basmati rice, cucumber cuts, rotis and the satini pomme d'amour.

Conclusion

Thank you for picking this book. This book contains recipes which are more healthful and based on alkaline diet. These contain eggs, fruit, vegetables and meat. A body that follows an alkaline diet may benefit from a variety of healthy advantages. So try to prepare at home and enjoy.